CREATIVE PROBLEM
IN THE FIELD

Creative Problem Solving in the Field
Reflections on a Career

William Foote Whyte

ALTAMIRA
PRESS

A Division of Sage Publications, Inc.
Walnut Creek • London • New Delhi

mi dwood

For information address:

AltaMira Press
A Division of Sage Publications, Inc.
1630 North Main Street, Suite 367
Walnut Creek, CA 94596

SAGE Publications Ltd.
6 Bonhill Street
London EC2A 4PU
United Kingdom

SAGE Publications India Pvt. Ltd.
M-32 Market
Greater Kailash 1
New Delhi 110 048 India

PRINTED IN THE UNITED STATES OF AMERICA

Library of Congress Cataloging-in-Publication Data
  Whyte, William Foote, 1914–
  Creative problem solving in the field : reflections on a career / by William Foote Whyte
    p. cm.
  Includes bibliographical references and index.
  ISBN 0–7619–8920–X (cloth : acid-free paper). — ISBN 0–7619–8921–8 (pbk. : Acid-free paper)
  1. Sociology—Research—Methodology. 2. Sociology—Field work.
  3. Social sciences—Research—Methodology. 4. Social sciences—Field work. I. Title.
  HM48.W45 1997
  301′.07′23 — dc21   97–4912
                                                                 CIP

97   98   99   00   01   8   7   6   5   4   3   2   1

Production Services: Laura Anne Lawrie
Editorial Management: Brent Chapman
Cover Design: Brent Chapman

6|5|2000

TABLE OF CONTENTS

ABOUT THE AUTHOR

William Foote Whyte was born June 27, 1914 of professional father and grandfathers. He graduated with highest honors from Swarthmore College in 1936, majoring in economics. *Financing New York City* was published as a bulletin of the American Academy of Political and Social Science in 1935. That led to his Junior Fellowship at Harvard, 1936–40, and his Ph.D. at the University of Chicago in 1943. He was assistant professor of sociology at the University of Oklahoma in 1943. He was to return to Harvard in 1943 to do research on Italian culture and teach in the program for U.S. army troops to invade Italy, but that was aborted by an attack of polio. He was Assistant, then Associate, Professor of Sociology at the University of Chicago from 1944 to 1948, Professor of Organizational Behavior in the School of Industrial and Labor Relations at Cornell, 1948–1979, then Emeritus Professor with part-time employment as research director, Programs for Employment and Workplace Systems (PEWS).

He is past president of the American Sociological Association, Society for Applied Anthropology, and Industrial Relations Research Association, and is the author of a number of books on organizational behavior in industry and in agriculture and rural development. *Street Corner Society*, in its four editions from 1943 to 1993, has sold 265,000 copies. It is the bestselling book in sociology published before 1950—excluding textbooks and classics such as Max Weber, Emile Durkheim, and Karl Marx.

Making Mondragón: The Growth and Dynamics of the Worker Cooperative Complex (jointly authored by Kathleen King Whyte) is widely regarded by students of the cooperative movement as the best book yet written on the Basque cooperatives of Mondragón. *Participant Observer*, an autobiography, was published in 1994.

PREFACE

In my junior year in the Swarthmore Honors program, as a member of an economics seminar, I wrote a research paper on the finances of New York City. Professor Clair Wilcox thought so well of the paper that he urged me to do some further work on it so he could get Thorsten Sellin, editor for the American Academy of Political and Social Science, to consider it for publication. *Financing New York City* was published in 1935.

That early publication probably won for me the Junior Fellowship at Harvard. I started out thinking I was going to do a study of the economics of slum district home ownership and taxation.

Before I had begun, I was fortunate to encounter a man who became my mentor and informal teacher, social anthropologist Conrad M. Arensberg. After completing research of an Irish rural community, he returned to the Society of Fellows at Harvard. There he took a particular interest in me, helping to move me toward a socially oriented study. He emphasized the importance of documenting what I was doing by writing detailed notes of observations and interviews soon after the events and not then trying to sort out the important from the unimportant.

My four years at Harvard did not lead directly toward a doctoral degree because at that time the Junior Fellow was required to concentrate entirely on research. Studying informally with a social anthropologist, I was not then aware of previous sociological studies of slum districts, so I did not start with a review of the sociological literature. By the time I left Harvard to study for the doctorate at the University of Chicago, I had the draft of the manuscript for what turned out to be *Street Corner Society* in my trunk.

At the recommendation of Conrad Arensberg, I went to Chicago to study with social anthropologist W. Lloyd Warner. He then had a joint appointment in the departments of anthropology and sociology, so that did not determine which department I majored in. I found that there was considerable overlap in the requirements of each department, and each department had requirements for study that I was not interested in, but those requirements in anthropology (archaeology and physical anthropology) seemed harder to learn. Four years out of college, I was in a hurry to finish my graduate studies so I decided to become a sociologist. That decision was further eased by the presence of Everett C. Hughes in the Sociology Department. He was then engaged in a study of a French Canadian industrial city—which came to be considered an anthropological or sociological classic. Hughes and Warner were also close friends.

By the time I was preparing for my doctoral examinations, I had read up on the Chicago sociological literature on slum districts, so I was well prepared to be cross-examined by sociologists Louis Wirth and Herbert Blumer. Wirth asked me how I defined a slum district. I said it was an inner city district with a high concentration of poor people living in poor housing conditions, with inadequate opportunities for jobs. He told me that was an economic and physical description. He wanted a social description. I knew he wanted me to say that a slum was socially disorganized, but I had already found that my slum was indeed well structured but in ways that did not fit in with middle-class values.

I insisted that the social research problem was to discover the nature of social relations and not to label it in advance. In effect, I had found that ignorance of the previous sociological literature had turned out to be an advantage in this case. I had started doing an exploratory study and had only sharpened my focus as I began to be familiar with the lives of the boys on the street corner and with their linkages (or lack of linkages) with local politicians and racketeers.

From this intensive experience, I did not conclude that I should ignore the academic literature in any new study I undertook. I simply decided that I should strive to keep an open mind and not go to work with a preformulated set of hypotheses.

Throughout my research career, I have developed most of my ideas through confronting problems I encountered in the field. I began with studies in the Italian American slum district in the North End of Boston, reported in *Street Corner Society*. At the outset, I thought I was doing a total community study. I began with participant observational studies of gangs of young men who were hanging out on street corners. I became so absorbed in those studies that I abandoned any thought of studies of the family, religion, and economic organization. I found I was instead trying to understand the relationship between the young men on the street corner and the larger structures of the political and racket organizations.

In all of my studies, I have been concerned with linking particular individuals with groups and larger social structures. Throughout my efforts to build individual-to-group-to-organization linkages, I did not want to lose sight of particular individuals. I was indeed finding that sometimes a particular individual could help build and transform organizations.

In my years of studying industrial relations, I was going beyond the focus of individual/group/organization to focus particular attention on the conflicts and accommodations of the management organization with the unionized workers. When most of my colleagues were focusing attention on union-management conflict, I found myself looking for what were then the rare cases of cooperation.

In studies of rural community development in Latin America, I was focusing on power, conflict, and cooperation in quite different social and economic settings. And finally, in studies of the Mondragón cooperative complex in the Basque region of Spain, I was focusing on an extraordinary set of organizations designed to resolve conventional organizational conflicts and arrive at higher levels of cooperation. In that study, I was paying particular attention to the socially creative leadership of one man, the founder and shaper of the Mondragón cooperative complex.

I have aimed to contribute to knowledge and find ways to make what I was learning yield some benefits to human society. In other words, I aimed to do basic research and applied research at the same time. Since this has not been a common ambition among professors, I have had to find my own way to do it.

My Ph.D. is in sociology, with social anthropology as my minor field. I joined the Society for Applied Anthropology when it was first organized in 1941 and I edited its journal for a six year period in the 1950s. In Cornell's School of Industrial and Labor Relations, I worked for many years in the Department of Organizational Behavior, whose membership included social psychologists as well as sociologists. Lawrence K. Williams, a social psychologist, was my partner for many years in our Peruvian studies. In other field studies, I have collaborated with political scientists. My undergraduate major at Swarthmore College was economics, and I continue to be interested in economic factors in community and organizational development.

I have been committed to studying society through a broad ranging focus, not limiting myself to the theories and research methods of any single discipline. I have picked up theoretical ideas wherever they seemed to illuminate the field problems I was studying; I have adapted such ideas to my own purposes or, wherever adaptation did not lead to the solutions I was seeking, I have sought to create my own theoretical framework. The results of that process are presented in this book.

Since my own theoretical ideas have arisen largely out of my fieldwork experiences, in this book I have not set theory apart from research methods. Where field experiences have led me to develop theoretical ideas, I describe those ideas. Where my field experience has suggested new approaches to research methods, I describe those methods.

For the background of all that is to follow, it would seem logical to begin with a statement of my ideas on sociology as social science. I do not do so here because my ideas on sociology and social science have evolved and changed over many years, and I prefer to describe my present position after I have described my field experiences and my developing research methods over many years. Readers will find that statement in Chapter 12 on "Sociology as Social Science."

I begin with four chapters dealing with participant observation. Gaining access to the scenes you want to study naturally comes first. I follow with a chapter on systematic observation and recording of observations. Then comes a chapter on informal interviewing and finally one on evaluation of the written record of the results gained in participant observation.

In Chapter 5 and later chapters, I shift the focus from participant observation to indicate I do not consider it the only method to use—although skills in observation and interviewing can be used in any type of social research. In "Money and Motivation" I demonstrate one approach to the study of motivation by examining the reactions of workers to piece-rate systems of payment.

In "Socio-Technical Systems" I argue for the need to consider work organizations not only as social systems but also as technical systems.

In "Studying Culture and Intercultural Relations," focusing on comparisons between the United States and Peru, I go beyond presenting case studies to show the problems and possibilities of carrying out large scale studies over an extended period of years.

In Chapters 8 through 11 I deal with combining various research methods: survey research and intensive field interviewing and observation; and historical research combined with current field studies. I illustrate the latter point by summarizing a case study of the Mondragón cooperative complex in the Basque provinces of Spain.

Chapters 12 through 14 discuss the relations between basic and applied social research, and then describe the building of an applied research and consulting organization at Cornell.

The final chapter, "A Vision for Sociology and Society," seeks to pull together what I have learned from more than 50 years of fieldwork in order to show how research can be used to make sociology more relevant to the general public and to provide various examples of the practical uses of sociology.

I am not presenting these concepts and ideas as if they represented the current state of knowledge in the 1990s. In some cases they may seem out of date, since others have gone beyond me in further research along the same lines. I present them as a personal report of how my thoughts evolved through experience in the field. I believe that some of these ideas retain their validity in the 1990s, but I will leave it to readers to decide the value of what I have presented as a contribution to sociology or simply as a personal report on what William Foote Whyte has learned over so many years of fieldwork.

CHAPTER ONE
GAINING ACCESS TO THE FIELD

B efore you can decide what and how you will observe, you must find your way into the organization or community you want to study. In an industrial organization, gaining access can often be achieved simply through getting a job, but the nature of that job can limit or expand one's scope of observation. For example, in his several job experiences, Donald Roy's observational possibilities were strictly confined to what he could see and hear around his particular job—giving his observations great depth but limited scope (Roy, 1959). By contrast, Melville Dalton (1959) had a job that offered wide opportunities for moving around and interacting with a large number of workers. He had the responsibility to measure the output of workers in a large production department but he had no role in setting the piece rates, so his functions were entirely noncontroversial. His office was in the area of time study men and industrial engineers, which opened the way for informal interviews with them and with their supervisors.

In such job-based cases, neither fellow workers nor managers knew that the worker was trying to carry out research, although they might know that he or she was working to pay for a college education.

If you aim to enter the field with an open commitment to do research, you will generally have to have the assent of the chief gatekeeper in management. He or she will want to know what you want to find out, what you will (and won't) report to management—perhaps also what you might plan to publish. To gain access to my first industrial study, I mistakenly agreed to give management clearance for the book I hoped to write. When I submitted *People in Petroleum* to the chief personnel man in Phillips

Petroleum, after a long delay he replied that he and his associates had learned much from my study but that it would not be in the interests of the company to permit it to be published.

That mistake could have been avoided. If the Phillips people had asked me about publication plans—I volunteered the commitment without being asked—I could have replied that anything I wrote would not identify the company. In fact (Whyte, 1965, 1969) that is what I later did in using cases from "Blank Oil Company."

The general lesson to be drawn from this mistake is to avoid advance commitments but, if management raises the issue, to say that you will make every effort to avoid identifying any individuals or the company in what you publish. If management people expect some feedback on the study, this could be arranged in an informal discussion meeting with them. If a union is involved in the case, the same commitment can be made to them.

As a general rule, I would expect management people to be more concerned about the immediate problems of observation and interviewing—how that can be fitted into the regular work routines of production. If you wish to take workers off the job for interviews, that costs management substantial money so would be more difficult to arrange. Otherwise, interviews can be arranged with workers after they get off work or in their homes, but there the extra costs are borne by the researchers.

If you are planning a study of a community or some part of a community, you may be able to move into that community. That is only the first step; being physically inside does not guarantee you access to the information you are seeking. For that purpose, you will need informal sponsorship from one or more gatekeepers, having a strong base in that part of the community. It may take you some time to find these people, but patience and persistence will pay off. In the North End of Boston, it was a social worker in a settlement house who arranged for me to meet "Doc" (Ernest Pecci), the leader of a corner gang of men in their twenties that hung out on a corner where the settlement house was located. Through Doc, I was introduced to the corner-boy world, and that led to a strong base from which I could branch out to make my own contacts.

Eliot Liebow (1967) found his base in *Tally's Corner*, a carry-out shop run by Tally. Elijah Anderson (1978) found his base in a neighborhood liquor store, which was an informal gathering place for young men in this area. Once inside, the researcher still needs to learn how to behave in this unfamiliar setting but that learning can be facilitated by asking the gatekeeper for advice and guidance.

Ruth Horowitz (1983) had no such informal sponsorship when she began hanging out on a Chicago area street to get acquainted with the young Chicano men and women in that area. She was not Chicana herself but Jewish, yet she was fluent in Spanish, which helped. Young women were not accustomed to hang out on the street in this area, yet Horowitz managed to make the position work for her, showing an interest about everything that was going on and avoiding any amorous relations with the young men and yet trying to be friendly with everyone. Eventually her persistence paid off and she came to know many of the young men and women and their families as a friend and confidant.

How do people get used to having you around? With any new group, at first I felt ill at ease. I sensed that they did not want me around, but, unless they told me to go away (which they never did), I remained until I was comfortable with them and they with me.

How do you explain the purposes of your study to the people in your neighborhood? I began with an elaborate story that I wanted to study the history of the neighborhood, to understand how the past shaped the present. When I used that story a couple of times, it left people glassy-eyed, not knowing what to think. I soon discovered that acceptance of my study depended on people's reaction to me. If Bill Whyte was all right, then my study must be all right. If I was not accepted as a person, then nothing could make my study acceptable. Furthermore, people needed time to get used to having me around, so I had to concentrate first on fitting in before I asked any questions.

It is important to make it clear that you are not trying to pass judgment on the people you meet. You are trying to understand them—in their own terms. In other words, you want to be accepted as a friend. As they come to accept you, you can assess what they expect from friends and to what extent you can meet their expectations.

CHAPTER TWO

SYSTEMATIZING PARTICIPANT OBSERVATION

Participant observation should not be a set of random activities. If you aim to establish patterns of interactions and activities that others can check and build on, you must try to go beyond personal impressions to *systematize* your observations. Only in that way will you be able to discover uniformities of behavior that others can check, verify or adapt to their own uses.

My approach places structure first, then focuses on the contents conveyed, and finally presents an overall interpretation of this sequence of behaviors. How this is done I will discuss in the next chapter on interviewing.

Where did the ideas underlying this approach come from?

When I began my four-year period (1936–1940) as a Harvard Junior Fellow, Conrad Arensberg, also a member of the Society of Fellows, had already completed his first major fieldwork in his studies of Irish rural society. Working with Eliot D. Chapple, they were developing a method for the study of interpersonal interactions. They were aiming to develop a theory and research methods that provided for the gathering of concrete and observable behavioral data—a framework that would withstand the criticisms of hard nosed natural scientists.

The first point Arensberg impressed on me was that the everyday activities of whatever people I was with constituted important data for research. I should therefore write in full detail what I observed. That advice served me well, as later I would be able to use notes for purposes I had not expected at the time of observation.

Let us assume that you are observing an informal group or a group in a work situation. What behaviors can you observe and record systematically? Let us focus on the most elementary things. Interactions: who interacts with whom, for how long and how frequently? Activities: what are the people doing together—from informal social activities to work group activities? What interactions precipitate a change in group activities? It is observations such as these that provide essential clues to the structure of the group—and understanding the group structure is essential to understanding individual behavior.

Chapple developed the interaction chronograph, a machine that allows observers to record in time the conversation between two or more people: who dominates the discussion, who interrupts whom, who continues after an interruption, and who speaks first after a silence. With myself as the only observer on the street corner, I could not use that method. Nevertheless, I adapted their approach to my own situation.

I found that the key to understanding group structure is distinguishing between *pair events*, interactions between two individuals, and *set events*, interactions among three or more individuals in the Chapple-Arensberg terminology. In a group of three or more individuals, the one who initiates a change in activities is the leader. If the group remains together and interacts frequently for an extended period of time, these leadership patterns come to be stabilized. If a stable pattern does not emerge, this is because the group has not been long enough together or because its leadership is shifting.

To illustrate with the group I knew best in *Street Corner Society*, Doc was the leader. He was the one who initiated changes in group activities or endorsed the suggestion of one of the other members. If a member suggested a change that Doc did not endorse, no change in group activities took place.

Doc's leadership position could also be observed through the spatial position of the members, as their positions changed through time. Often some members were on the street corner, interacting in subgroups of two or three men, without any general conversation linking them. When Doc arrived, the whole group of 10 to 13 members reshaped itself around Doc. When Doc spoke, the others listened to him. When another member spoke but noticed that Doc was not paying attention to him, he would stop, pause, and then try again to get Doc's attention.

The same observations revealed the rankings of men when Doc was not present. Doc's closest friends were Danny, Mike, and Long John, his fellow members in the leadership subgroup. Danny or Mike would then assume leadership of the group. (Long John never assumed the leadership role; his position in the group was ambiguous—a close friend of Doc but not otherwise respected.)

Below the leadership subgroup were three subgroups. Each one had its own leader: the initiator of activity changes or the endorser of changes proposed by others.

This method served to delineate the ranking structure of men standing on the street corner. For people sitting around tables and chairs in a club room, the mapping of spatial positions provides the initial evidence of subgroups—of patterns of association among club members. In my study of the Cornerville Social and Athletic Club, I was able to chart these spatial positions on two or more occasions every night. I did not make notes while watching, but withdrawing into the toilet provided some opportunity for note-taking, which I later filled out in our apartment, across the street from the club.

This method demonstrated that there were two large groups in the club—people sitting together and interacting—and that there were a few men who interacted with each group. I set out to find the leader of the club, and I found there was no such person. Each large group or faction had its own leader, and the president of the club was simply someone agreeable to both sides but otherwise having no power to initiate anything on his own.

When behavioral scientists are often happy when they achieve a statistical correlation of .30, which means that they have accounted for 9 percent of the variance, it seems a wild idea to suggest that anyone has developed any 100 percent discriminating measure, but that is the case with the analysis of *set events*.

When three or more people get together and remain together for frequent periods of interactions and activities, a stable relationship develops. The leader is the one who either directly initiates new activities or else approves suggestions and proposals of others. When someone makes a suggestion that is not supported by the leader, we observe no change in group activities. In my experience, this is a generalization which holds true except for the following two situations, (a) the group has not been meeting long enough for a stable pattern to evolve, or (b) the leadership is in the process of change.

21

I began with these theoretical and methodological ideas. In a meeting in the early 1950s, psychologist Arthur Kornhouser commented, "It is surprising how far Bill Whyte has gotten with such a simple minded theoretical framework." I believed that simplicity can be a virtue if it focuses on common patterns of interaction and activities.

This simpleminded approach to the study of interaction has almost entirely been neglected by sociologists for all the years since I used it in the late 1930s. The predominant focus on interaction has been in terms of the study of *symbolic interaction* (Blumer, 1969). This means that sociologists have been concentrating on analyzing the symbolic meanings of the words, expressions, and gestures that accompany discussions and conversations. That is indeed a more challenging intellectual task than counting and recording frequencies of interactions and initiations of changes in activities, but the intellectual challenge can lead to a wide range of symbolic interpretations, without any way of determining which one is most likely to be valid.

The counting of interactions, together with the recording of spatial positions among those interacting, is a low skilled operation that would seem boring to many sociologists, but it should be regarded as a critically important aspect of any study of interaction. That method provides the evidence for charting the social structure of the group being observed. If we understand the informal positions of group members, our analysis of the symbolic aspects of interaction should be much more valid.

———————————————————————

That type of structural analysis served me very well in studying informal groups on the street corner. After completing that study, I felt I needed to go on to study the larger social structures in the neighborhood and to find out how they were linked with street corner gangs.

I had learned enough about the social structure of the North End to recognize that there were two large organizational systems: the racket organization that controlled a daily lottery of numbers that paid off to winners; and the political organization.

I got my first lead to the racket organization when a friend told me he had had to buy two tickets to a banquet celebrating the son of the local police captain having passed his bar examination. His wife did not want to go. Would I like to go with him? I knew what sorts of people would be there: policemen, local politicians, and members of the racket organization, so I was happy to accept.

While we were spending a long time waiting for the banquet to be served, my friend introduced me to Tony Lucido, a member of middle management of the racket organization—he had runners who sold numbers and turned the slips over to him and he took his cut and passed them on to "the office." We then spent some time bowling and then got together over dinner.

Tony had seen me the past summer taking pictures of the saints day "festas." We talked about that for a while, and then I found that he lived within a block of where my own flat was. When that did not lead to a closer relationship, I spent some time with his brother who ran a corner store, where some numbers were sold. When I found that Tony was a member of a club across the street of our own flat, I also joined that club. That opened the way to my study of the racketeer in the Cornerville Social and Athletic Club.

At first I had avoided involvement with any political faction so as not to be limited by those ties in getting to work with others. When local state senator Joseph Langone was supporting the campaign for mayor of James M. Curley, who was widely popular throughout the district, I volunteered to work with Langone's people. Later, when Langone became a candidate for congress and had no local opposition, I again signed on as a volunteer. They did not know what to do with me, but I proposed to take notes on committee meetings, discussing campaign strategies. I turned the notes over to the candidate's wife, Tina, and kept a carbon copy.

I never did get invited to any meetings with the real power figures, but I was close enough to the scene to pick up much information about what was going on. For example, once Tina said to me in passing, "Bill, let's face it. When we really want to win, we go to the racketeers." Langone had not had any racketeer backing in his campaigns for the state senate, but for campaigns involving large areas he could not reach personally, he had to depend on the racket organization which had its members everywhere.

In working with the political organizations and the local racketeers, I was building my analysis of the relations between the corner boys and the larger organizational structures. I had to develop new roles for myself in order to fit myself into these new structures. For this process, I claim no special creativity. First I had to know where I wanted to go and then figure out how to get there. That would take a great deal of patience and a small amount of resourcefulness. If the fieldworker keeps looking for opportunities, they will eventually manifest themselves.

CHAPTER THREE

INTERVIEWING IN THE FIELD

Interviewing should be seen as part of the whole fieldwork process, rather than as an isolated exercise. If the interview is in the first stages of a study of an organization or community, you do not start out by trying to set up appointments to do interviews. People need time to get used to having a participant observer around and to feel that they can trust the researcher not to do anything to harm them.

As a participant observer, most of your interviewing will be done informally, simply listening to what people are saying and sometimes asking them to explain how they feel about the situation they are describing.

When you are well established in your relations with a particular group, it may be helpful to get a key informant aside, to sit around a table for an extended period of time—an hour or so—in order to explore thoroughly the informant's experience and views on topics of key interest to your research. At that point, it may even be possible to get the informant's permission to tape the interview, but, even with permission, this formalization of the process may inhibit the free expression by the informant.

The field interview has sometimes been referred to as nondirective, but, for my purposes, that is a misnomer. I see the process as freely structured, not following any set form of questions yet focusing on certain themes important to the researcher. That means being alert for responses that suggest new angles to explore, that may turn out to be more important than anything the researcher had in mind before the interview.

The interview generally should follow certain guidelines: not to argue with the informant, not to express disapproval of him or her, and not to interrupt the statements made—with the exception of the occasional informant who would seem to go on forever going over the same ground. In that case, it is important to be able to interrupt gracefully—which should not be difficult because that is the way most people try to communicate with nonstop talkers. For studies of attitudes in an organization or community, the questionnaire survey is the appropriate instrument. For the field interview, you are only interested in how the person's experience led him or her to form the attitudes in question. When the informant expresses a particular attitude, you follow up with a question about what experiences led to the formation of that attitude or set of attitudes.

How do you make a record of what the informant says? If you tape record the interview, and have a research grant for secretarial assistance, you can ask your secretary to transcribe it. If you have no secretary, you can transcribe it yourself, but that is a long and arduous task, so you will usually find that you will want to transcribe only certain key interviews or a few parts of a particular interview.

If you have not tape-recorded the interview, you will have to write down later what you are able to remember. When I first tried this, I could remember very little, but nevertheless I wrote down everything I could. At the end of a day in the field, I would make notes on the interviews and the following morning type them out. I could never claim that I had recorded everything the informant said, but when s/he made a strong positive or negative statement about anybody or any thing, I could be almost certain that my quotation was correct.

In my North End study, I had opportunities to go over what an informant said to me with Doc and with Chick Morelli, the leader of the college boys club, and neither one claimed I had misquoted him—though Chick did say that I made him sound too much like a corner boy.

Depending on your relations with particular informants, you may find it useful to take your write-up of the interviews to them. You can then ask: have I remembered correctly, have I left anything significant out—and do you now have anything to add?

That was the procedure followed by Frank Wayno in his study of the transformation of the Xerox Corporation (see Chapter 12). There he began with considerable background on the company and the union, from previous studies by other Cornellians. He knew that management and union leaders took great pride in what had been accomplished, so he faced no problems of access and informant cooperation. He had identified in advance some of the key figures in this transformation. As he interviewed them, they pointed out others that he should interview.

The informants wrote extensive notes on their interview transcription, which helped Wayno to decide on next steps in interviewing or analysis.

The foregoing discussion applies only to the individual interview, by far the most common type. You may find it useful to set up group interviews, recognizing that there are things said in a one-person interview that would not be said—at least in the same way—in a group situation. In their study of the FAGOR cooperative group in the Mondragón complex, Davydd Greenwood and associates within FAGOR (Greenwood & Gonzalez, 1989) set up panels of eight members representing differences in experience: old timers and those recently hired, high and low status levels, and different occupations (production and maintenance worker, technician and engineer).

In each case, a moderator conducted the discussion but only served to start the group discussing some general issue: is there some value added to working for a cooperative instead of a private firm; how do you evaluate the degree of participation and communication in your cooperative?

This process revealed some important findings that did not come out in individual interviews. From the individual interviews, the researchers had assumed that the low level of participation was due to member apathy. On the contrary, the group interviews made it clear that the members wanted to participate more but did not find the existing channels and procedures conducive to effective participation.

They also found that, in the individual interviews, the informants expressed themselves more negatively about management and management policies than they did in the group interviews. In the group setting, a negative view expressed by one person was always balanced by a favorable comment by another member. Nor was this balancing caused by concern with management's reaction, for the managers would not know who made what comments.

In summary, the interview is an essential complement to group observation. The researcher needs to distinguish the initial access interviews from those that follow when the researcher is more familiar with the situation and the interviewees are more familiar with the researcher.

In participant observation, most of the interviews will be conducted highly informally. As later interviews are done, the researcher should be able to probe more deeply and even set up times and places for interviews.

The researcher should recognize the differences between individual and group interviews, experimenting with different approaches to see what fits best with the purposes of the study.

If you carry out a large number of interviews with the same group or organization, you will need to develop an indexing system so that you will be readily able to quote what you want to use in later writing. Long before the age of computers, I developed my own system. I numbered the interviews on the dates carried out and typed in the names of the person or persons interviewed, the names of those mentioned in the interview, and a brief notation of the topics discussed. In the case of the group I knew best, the Nortons, my notes ran to eight pages. Reading those eight pages several times, I could keep in mind the location of anything I might want to quote. Later, in my studies of the restaurant industry, I added notes on relationships discussed: for example, hostess-waitress, service supervisor-manager, and so on.

With today's technology, it is possible to accelerate and simplify the process. I cannot speak from personal experience, but colleague Sally Klingel reports that "most of the word processing software now has an indexing function. The newer versions of WordPerfect and Word both have it. You simply mark words in the text and the software automatically creates the index with page numbers."

The software does the unskilled part of the job. It remains for the researcher to apply professional skills to create the indexing items in the first place.

CHAPTER FOUR

FACTS, INTERPRETATIONS, AND ETHICS IN QUALITATIVE INQUIRY

To what extent can we consider a report of qualitative research as factual? I thought I knew the answer to that question until the recent surge of interest in critical epistemology, deconstructionism, and postpositivism. I had to face these new trends when the *Journal of Contemporary Ethnography* (21:1 1992) ran a special issue to evaluate *Street Corner Society*.

That issue arose out of an article W. A. Marianne Boelen submitted to the *Journal*. She had gone back to the North End of Boston on several occasions 30 to 45 years after I left it in 1940, had interviewed some of the people I knew and some others, and had written an interpretation quite different from mine. That issue contained my rejoinder and discussions of the controversy by three behavioral scientists, anthropologist Arthur Vidich and sociologists Laurel Richardson and Norman Denzin.

I had assumed that the assignment of the behavioral science critics was to rule whether my account or Boelen's was more likely to be an accurate description and interpretation of the North End in the late 1930s, but none of them took a position on that issue. Vidich praised the book, but then simply stated that "readers may draw their own conclusions about the issues raised in these essays" (p.80).

Richardson and Denzin bypassed that issue, claiming that the nature of the critical game had changed since I did the study. As Richardson put it

> The core of this postfoundational climate is *doubt* that any discourse has a privileged place, any text an authoritative "corner" on the truth. (p. 104)

Denzin called me a "positivist-social realist" (p. 130) and stated that

today, social realism is under attack. It is now seen as but one narrative strategy for telling stories about the world out there. (p. 126)

As the 20th century is now in its last decade, it is appropriate to ask if we any longer want this kind of social science that Whyte produced and Boelen, in her own negative way endorses? (p. 131)

The deconstructionist attack surprised me. It seemed to me that Denzin and Richardson made no distinction between facts and fiction. His later report in the journal *Qualitative Inquiry* (June 1996) leads off with a quotation from a novelist, E. L. Doctorow:

There is no longer any such thing as fiction or nonfiction, there is only narrative.

I insist that there are such things as *physical and social facts* and that Boelen was demonstrably wrong on many facts. A few examples: In my book, I called Boston Eastern City. She called it Easter City. She claimed that the common language on the street corner was Italian. Among the many corner gangs I knew in 1940, I never heard any Italian spoken except for an occasional swear word. These men had either been born here or had immigrated as small children and then had gone through school here. She noted that my wife's parents were popular with the restaurant people I had lived with before marriage because they did not speak English. One of Alice King's ancestors came over on the Mayflower. One of Clarence King's ancestors fought with Ethan Allen at the Battle of Ticonderoga. And so on.

Boelen must also be faulted for failing to live up to well-established standards for criticism: she quoted me from my book out of context. She claimed that I had distorted the interpretation of the district to conform to the theoretical interpretation of the University of Chicago sociology department. I had written that, after going to Chicago, I had immersed myself in the Chicago sociology's slum literature. She fails to quote the sentence that immediately follows in which I state that I found this literature "garbage" and did not let it influence my interpretation. In fact, in my doctoral examination, I was hard pressed by two of my examiners because I refused to call Boston's North End a disorganized community.

I also was surprised that Richardson and Denzin failed to recognize the difference between my detailed notes, typed the same day or the day after, and the recollections of selected subjects 30 to 45 years after the events in question. To Denzin, I told one narrative and Boelen told another; there was no standard enabling a critic to choose between them.

With the publication of the second edition of SCS in 1955, containing my appendix on my experiences in making the study, I began to hear people speak of the book as "a sociological classic." It was not until the *Journal of Contemporary Ethnography* published its critique that the book came under attack. In that journal and then in the 1993 fourth edition of SCS, and finally in an article in the journal of *Qualitative Inquiry* (June 1996), I replied to the critics.

I don't want to deal further with the Boelen attack because an account of what 17 informants told her of their memories of me and my study 30 to 45 years after I left the district hardly merits the attention it has received.

That leaves two issues remaining: the deconstructionist critique and questions raised about my ethics by Laurel Richardson.

While I do not claim that every detail in my book is accurate, I made every attempt to get my facts straight. It seems to me that the deconstructionist critique fails to recognize the distinction between fact and fiction. I argue that there are such things as *social and physical facts*. The researcher must begin by getting those facts straight. How the researcher interprets the behavior of those observed and studied in relation to those facts is certainly subject to argument. If the critic is demonstrably wrong on a number of those physical and social facts, as Boelen was, then the interpretations based on them must have little validity.

By the deconstructionist logic, I see no way of utilizing qualitative inquiry to build a social science. I have therefore concluded that those embracing deconstructionism are advancing along a dead-end street.

The best refutation of deconstructionism was recently presented by New York University physicist Alan Sokal, who perpetrated a hoax on the deconstructionists with his article entitled "Transgressing the Boundaries: Toward a Transformative Hermaneutics of Quantum Gravity." According to *The New York Times* (May 20, 1996), Sokal submitted the hoax to the journal *Social Text*, which embraces postpositivism cultural criticism, and that journal published it as if it were a serious scholarly article.

The fact that the editorial board of *Social Text* mistook a parody for a scholarly contribution indicates the morass these new cultural thinkers have got themselves into. I prefer to ignore them to get on with my own work.

The Richardson critique raises questions that deserve answers. On research methods, how could I quote informants at length without having a tape recorder to get their exact words?

At first, when I tried to remember what was said, I could hardly bring anything back. With continued practice, my memory steadily improved. I would make brief notes on what I remembered as soon as I could after the encounter and then write it up in detail as soon as I could get to my typewriter. Of course, I do not claim that every word is correct, but I could be almost certain that when the informant made a strong statement for or against somebody or something, I could quote those exact words.

When Doc read the first draft of the book, he had a number of criticisms and suggestions, but he did not question any of my recording of his words. As I reported in the book (page 341), at times he would say "This will embarrass me, but this is the way it was so go ahead with it." He seemed as determined as I to get the facts straight.

Several years after the book was published, I called on Chick Morelli, the leader of the Italian Community Club, to ask him what he thought of it. He acknowledged that I had my facts straight but said I should remember they were young then and he had changed much since that time. On my recordings of his words, his only criticism was that I made him sound too much like a corner boy. When I discussed these reactions with Doc, he suggested that perhaps reading the book had helped Chick to change; few people have such an opportunity to see themselves as others see them.

Richardson's questions on professional ethics involved my identification of particular individuals in the text. By the time of publication in 1981 of the third edition of *SCS*, I thought it would add interest to the book if I revealed that Cornerville was the North End of Boston and identified some of the chief characters. Ernest Pecci (Doc) had died in 1967, so nothing I did could hurt him now. Since most students who read the book find Doc an interesting and admirable character, it did not occur to me that members of his family might object. I did make an effort to reach his sons, but none of my North End contacts knew where they were.

I later heard that they claimed they had been "subject to ridicule and harassment by their friends and family in the greater Boston area." That strikes me as a gross exaggeration.

If I had not identified Doc, that would have solved the problem for Pecci's sons. There would, however, have remained a problem of those still living in the area who could have recognized themselves in the book. *SCS* was never reviewed in any Boston newspaper, but the North End branch library displayed on its bulletin board, under the label of "Recent Books of Interest," Kathleen's book jacket for *Street Corner Society*—and that book jacket remained there for several years. Since the library building was on the corner where Doc and his gang hung out, the members could hardly have been unaware of it.

I assumed that some people would be embarrassed by reading how they were portrayed in the book, but I can't believe that I did anyone any serious harm. In fact, I did know some damaging information about some individuals that I did not reveal so as to avoid doing harm.

Could I have avoided embarrassing or risking harm to anybody and still have communicated what I wanted to communicate? I think it would have been possible if I had confined myself to writing a series of articles for academic journals.

That would not have satisfied me nor would what I wanted to say reach a broader public. I believed that the themes I was presenting would have a greater impact if I could present them about particular individuals, their relations with each other, the relations of group to group, and groups to larger organizations. I did want the book to be read widely, as it has been. Others can evaluate better than I what impact the book has had on the teaching of sociology, anthropology, and social work—and on the understanding of those who read *SCS*.

In stressing the interests of the subjects of the study, Richardson fails to consider the rights an author should have to report on what he or she has found. No one-sided focus on the interests of the subjects reflects the reality sociologists and social anthropologists face in dealing with the real world we seek to report.

If I had to do it all over again, what changes would I make? I would not have identified any individuals with their real names. I knew I could not hurt Doc, long dead, but it never occurred to me that his sons would be upset. Leaving out real names would not have weakened my report in any way.

I don't believe my book was widely read in the North End, but the Nortons obviously became aware of it, and some of them read enough in it to recognize their own characters. They did not like my ranking of the Nortons, with some of them confined among the followers. One of them insisted that, while Doc was respected, the leader was Nutsy and not Doc.

Clearly some people were embarrassed by the book, but I could not find any evidence that I had seriously damaged any of them.

The embarrassment of a few people may be a necessary price to pay for an intensive participant observer report that has been read by thousands of college students and others in the general public. Many college professors have made the book required reading. Years after the book was published, I would be approached by strangers at American Sociological Association meetings, who wanted to know "What has happened to Doc?"

CHAPTER FIVE
TRANSACTIONAL RELATIONSHIPS

In my initial interaction framework, I had concentrated on quantitative analysis of interactions. In the early 1950s my field experience had led me to see the need to deal with some aspects of symbolic interaction. That led to my framework of *transactional relationships*, focusing on the way relationships yielded benefits or penalties to the interacting parties.

I was trying to discover relationships between interactions, and activities, and interpersonal sentiments or attitudes. At first I was reassured by the formulation by George C. Homans of the relationship between interaction and interpersonal sentiments (Homans, 1950). Homans posited a simple relationship in which increasing frequencies and durations of interpersonal interactions generated increasingly favorable sentiments among members of the group—up to some point.

That proposition exploded in my face, when I spent some weeks with the National Training Laboratory for Group Development in the summer program in Bethel, Maine in 1950. With five research collaborators (Whyte, 1953), I was studying six discussion groups of about 21 members each, which met every afternoon for 2 hours over a period of 3 weeks. The explicit purpose of the discussions was to help members develop ideas and projects designed to solve "back home problems." In five out of the six groups we observed, increasing frequency and duration of interpersonal interactions generated substantial conflict among the members.

That prompted me to rethink the relationship between interactions and interpersonal sentiments among different informal groups on the street corner. The Bethel groups were established by those administering the training program. While members were free to limit their participation in the discussion, their organizations had paid for this training experience, and no one felt free to leave the group altogether. On the street corners, if an individual did not fit into the group, he either could voluntarily withdraw or be, in effect, rejected by various pressures of other group members. Thus the relationship between interpersonal sentiments and interactions held true of the street corner because this was a voluntary and self constituted group. There was no reason to assume that groups constituted by people in authority in training programs or in industry or business would evidence such a pattern.

This revelation led me to reformulate the relationship so that increasing frequency of interaction would intensify interpersonal sentiments but would not determine whether they would be positive or negative. I was groping for a relationship between interactions and rewards and punishments associated with the interactional relationship—reinforcements, as the psychologists would call them.

I began with the distinction between *intrinsic* and *extrinsic* satisfactions derived (or expected) from the particular interactional relationship. The *intrinsic* satisfactions are those that the participants in the interactions derive out of the process of being together and conversing and taking action together. The *extrinsic* satisfactions are those derived (or expected) are those that the parties gain in terms of some concrete or symbolic rewards.

I assume that unless they derive some enjoyment through interacting with the other party or at least find those interactions personally tolerable, the relationship will tend to break down, however much the parties had expected to get out of the interactional relationship. This means that *intrinsic* satisfactions are important—but not all important. Sociologists and social psychologists have created a large and useful research literature on the relationship between interactions and *intrinsic* satisfactions, but the relationships between interaction and *extrinsic* satisfactions has only been partially explored.

In my terms, only one type of *transactional relationship* has been explored thoroughly by sociologists and social psychologists, who focus on what they call exchange theory. This came into vogue around the end of the nineteenth century with the publication by the French social anthropologist, Marcel Mauss of *The Gift* (1954 English translation). The contributions of Alvin Gouldner (1960), George C. Homans (1961), and Peter Blau (1955) have brought the analysis of interpersonal reciprocities to the forefront of behavioral science theorizing. In fact, some sociologists were assuming that interpersonal reciprocity was the primary or only force keeping societies together.

Through my experience in the Trumansburg Rotary Club, I began to see the costs and limitation of exchange. We met every Thursday night in a restaurant. Before the meeting, many of the members stopped at the bar for drinks. When I entered, a friend would spot me before I reached the bar and order and pay for a scotch and soda for me. I was pleased by this friendly recognition, but then I did not want to sponge off my friends. I decided to come in early and order up a drink for my friend before he got to the bar. That was no solution. We finished our drinks before dinner, and then he ordered and paid for a second drink for both of us. I did not want two drinks before dinner, but now I had to drink and pay for two. There was no way out until I changed my schedule to come in just at dinner time and avoid all drinks.

As I reflected on this experience, I realized other limitations to interpersonal reciprocity. It could not be extended indefinitely. There is a limitation to the number of interpersonal reciprocities that any individual can maintain. This relationship can be an important building block for any political organization, but, in a business organization, it poses hazards as well as advantages. Building business primarily on friendship can lead to inefficiency and failure.

If exchange was not the only force operating to structure human relations, what other forces were there? I began to construct my own typology.

I began with exchange, but, in my typology, I called it *positive exchange* to allow for its opposite, *negative exchange*, when two parties are engaged in penalizing each other and then trying to "get even"—also a very common and powerful transactional relationship.

There must be other forces shaping human relations beyond interpersonal reciprocity. Searching for those other forces led me to develop a system of seven transactional relationships. I will present that list, in summary form, beginning with what I call elementary types:

1. *Positive exchange*. The exchange of favors, in alternating form: you do me a favor and later I reciprocate by doing you a favor.
2. *Trading: the buy-sell relationship*: from barter to cash and credit transactions.

3. *Competition.* Here individuals or groups are competing with each other to gain some financial or prestige awards. We should, however, distinguish between *zero-sum* and *positive sum* competition. In *zero-sum* competition, there is only one winner and everybody else loses. In *positive sum* competitions, there can be many winners—for example, in a nationwide competition for school examinations, pupils in one school can increase the possibilities that one of their school mates will win a prize through working together in studying. In this situation, cooperation can pay off.

4. *Negative Exchange.* Here individuals or groups become involved in a tit-for-tat contest: you do something against their interests and they respond in kind.

5. *Open conflict.* Both individuals or groups openly acknowledge that they are trying to damage each other. Those relations can include physical combat or various forms of litigation.

   Such elementary types often occur in pure form. They can, however, occur in combination to make up several complex types, as follows.

6. *Authority.* In one respect, this is similar to the *Trading* transactional relationship: the person in authority agrees to pay other people specified amounts to do work. In *Trading*, if either the buyer or the seller is not satisfied with the deal, they simply will stop trading with each other. The *Authority* relationship is designed to continue for an extended period of time and is often supported by contractual agreements and regulated to some extent by the state. How that complex relationship works out is the focus of much of the organizational behavior literature.

7. *Joint-Payoff.* In this type, two or more individuals or groups agree to pool some of their resources in order to gain resources from the environment. That is, they do not gain or lose directly from dealing with each other—as in *Positive Exchange*, *Trading*, *Negative Exchange*, and *Authority* relations—but rather from external sources.

   Joint-Payoff is the basis of organization in partnerships in business and the professions and is one of the guiding principles of worker cooperatives. It also frequently occurs in informal collaborative relations between individuals or groups. It is frequently accompanied by *Positive Exchange*. It can also be combined with the *Authority* relationship. For example, in increasing numbers we see unions and managements getting together to develop systems whereby the gains achieved are shared between the union and the company.

I see important opportunities for organizational progress in combining *Joint-Payoffs* with *Multi-Objective* planning. Economists have given much attention to the analysis of scarcity, comparing objectives in terms of trade-offs and opportunity costs, that is, what you give up in doing one thing through not being able to do something else at the same time. That principle, however, applies only to *actions*, not to *objectives*. Frequently several objectives can be reached through the same line of action. Economists also recognize "externalities" (Samuelson, 1967)—the additional valuable outcomes that can be produced in carrying out a project aimed at one principal objective. Sociologists have recognized this issue through discussing "unanticipated consequences of purposive social action" (Merton, 1936).

If we adopt a *Joint-Payoff* strategy, we are likely to be pushed toward *Multi-Objective* planning because we find that the other party or parties have some action objectives different from our own as well as objectives they share with us. To the extent that we can agree on a broader set of objectives, the project can greatly expand the possibilities of collaboration.

Such possibilities are explored in detail in Chapter 8.

————————————————◼•◼————————————————

What is the potential value of such a system of *transactional relationships*? It can serve two purposes, (a) help planners, managers, union leaders, and politicians to devise effective strategies, and (b) open up a new and promising area for further research.

The scheme can be modified, strengthened, or otherwise be improved through research focusing on the results achieved through emphasizing one objective versus pushing for another one. Research can also provide useful guidance for multi-objective planning by examination of the conditions for success of multi-objective strategies.

I define the nature of the transaction in terms of the intentions of the initiator to the transaction. Research can focus on the potential differences between what is proposed by A and the *perception* by B of that proposal. For example, if B does not trust A, then B is likely to assume that what A presents (in other words) as a Joint-Payoff transaction will turn out actually to harm B. In that case, we are dealing with a more general problem: how past events and personal perceptions have generated this distrust between them and what might be done to build a more trusting relationship.

In the case of deep-seated and intense antagonism between the parties, several proposals for a joint-payoff transaction may not be enough to create positive reactions. In the relations between individuals A and B, if we assume that A continues to give out indications of cooperative intentions, B eventually will catch on and respond in kind. On the other hand, past relations may have built up such a wall of mistrust that B construes A's actions as a deceptive trick to catch B off guard.

In this "frozen" situation, it may take unexpected words or actions from A to unfreeze the established pattern and convince B that a cooperative relationship is possible. We all have seen this done dramatically on an international scale when President Anwar Sadat of Egypt announced publicly that he would fly to Israel and speak of cooperation with the Knesset. (To be sure, this act was preceded by "feelers" by officials of both parties to smooth the way for the public demonstration.)

In my own fieldwork, I have encountered two cases in which key symbols paved the way for a shift from conflict to cooperation.

In the case of S. Buchsbaum and Company and the International Chemical Workers Union (Whyte et al., 1946), the transition occurred in the midst of a strike for recognition of the union. To break the strike, management was hiring "scabs" to cross the picket line. One morning a strike-breaker drove up to the plant, at high speed, right onto the sidewalk to get his people close to the plant door. As International Representative Sidney Garfield told me, the picketers wanted to turn the car over in the street, but he intervened to stop them, recognizing (as he said) the American respect for private property—while he joined in with the other strikers to beat up the picketers. The plant watchman saw the action and reported it to President Herbert Buchsbaum, who was duly impressed. He recalled that in a strike in 1935, the striking workers had thrown sand in the gears and committed other acts of sabotage. At least the current union was more responsible.

That was not enough to turn Buchsbaum around, but he had to recognize that he was now in a different legal situation. The Wagner Act had been passed and approved by the Supreme Court, so his lawyer told him he would have to meet with leaders of the striking union.

He had lunch with a business friend who had signed a contract with the union and with Samuel Laderman, union president. The friend told

Buchsbaum that he had nothing to fear from Laderman, that he was a man of his word—and a lover of opera. Buchsbaum did not care for opera himself but his wife loved the performances, and he recognized that opera lover did not fit with his perceptions of union leaders as either racketeers or communists.

When he met with International Representative Sidney Garfield and a group of his striking workers in his office, they asked him why he was against unions. He replied that it was because they restricted output and pressed for higher wages than the firm could pay. They countered with the claim that they wanted to raise production. "How could they do that," he asked. While he took notes, workers gave him examples of what they would be able to do. He saw thousands of dollars in savings annually in the examples raised. Those figures persuaded him. He now agreed to sign up with the union. Thus began a marked shift from conflict to cooperation.

The shift in relations in the case of the United Steelworkers and the Inland Steel Container Company came a year after the plant had been shut down with a bitter strike lasting 191 days. The key to the change was the entrance of a new International Representative, Jake Shafer. Without having been involved through the conflict period, he could make a fresh approach to negotiations. Thinking that another strike was inevitable, the local leaders were happy to turn over chief negotiation responsibilities to Shafer.

Instead of trying to place the blame on management, Shafer focused on current management issues, asking them why they felt as they did in each case. Instead of getting involved in a quick back-and-forth dialogue, he encouraged them to express their ideas freely and fully. Management responded similarly.

Shafer also introduced another tactic to take the heat out of the negotiations. One morning he arrived with a set of prints of photographs from a recent hunting and fishing trip. He had stopped into a drug store to pick them up on the way to the plant. Now he showed them around, as workers and managers related what they were seeing to their own experience. That tactic established a changed relationship between Shafer and Robert Novy, General Factories Manager. As Novy commented to me later, "It's been my experience that whenever you run into a real sportsman, you'll find that he is a pretty regular fellow. He's a man you can deal with straight from the shoulder. That's one of the things that sold me on Shafer." (Whyte, 1951)

In these two cases, it was symbolic words and actions such as Garfield's intervention to prevent the strikers from overturning the car of the strike breakers and Shafer's diversionary effort with his photographs of his hunting and fishing trips that eased the transition from conflict to cooperation. On the other hand, we must not overestimate the power of such symbols in keeping cooperative activities going. Unless the parties can move beyond the transition to consolidate the cooperative relationship with new activities that they do together, their activities may revert to the old pattern.

CHAPTER SIX

MONEY AND MOTIVATION

How do you do fieldwork in the study of human motivation? And how to you organize collaborative research in fieldwork?

In my own research and that of my associates, we concentrated on the responses of people to financial incentives (piece rates) in industry in the 1940s and 1950s.

In studies of agricultural research and development in the 1960s and 1970s, I focused on the responses of small farmers in Latin America to the incentives to change offered to them by agricultural researchers or extension agents.

For the first industry studies, I worked with three graduate students who had been participant observers in industry. Donald Roy and Orvis Collins had been factory production workers, paid on piece rates. Melville Dalton was then serving as a checker in a steel mill, with no responsibility for setting the piece rates, but in a job that left him free to converse with workers, time-and-motion-study men, accountants, and supervisors. To contribute from my own fieldwork, I did a study of a plantwide incentive system in Bundy Tubing Company.

If I could work with this three-man team, it occurred to me that we could write a book together on money and motivation in industry. We did write a number of chapters together, but somehow the book project did not work out at that time.

The project had its second beginning after I came to the School of Industrial and Labor relations at Cornell University in 1948. I describe it in this way in the preface to *Money and Motivation* (1955):

Conception occurred to me in my bathtub. I rarely take the *American Sociological Review* for bathtub reading, but this time I had it with me because I was interested in an article just published by Roy on "Work Satisfaction and Social Reward in Quota Achievement" (vol. XVIII, no. 5). I read the piece with mounting excitement and yet with some sense of regret. Wasn't it too bad, I told myself, that we had never been able to push to conclusion our book on incentives when there was so much rich data available? Suddenly the thought struck me that perhaps the book had already been partially written. Perhaps it would now be possible to take the published material we had and, with relatively little additional effort, make this the book we once had hoped to write.

I had underestimated seriously the time and effort needed to put together what we had, to look then at the pattern, and to see what had yet to be filled in. I organized the project, edited the chapters, and did much of the writing, but the book is a thoroughly collaborative project with my collaborators furnishing copy and ideas for new cases to be included and sharing in the royalties. The coauthors now included a combination of my Chicago collaborators and those working with me at Cornell: Collins, Dalton, and Roy and Friedrich Fuerstenberg, Frank Miller, Leonard Sayles, George Strauss—plus Alex Bavelas at M.I.T., who described a case to then student Strauss.

What did I learn from this project—beyond an intimate knowledge of worker and manager behavior with piece-rate systems? Theoretically, I picked up ideas from psychologist B. F. Skinner (1971), who expressed the essence of *operant conditioning* most succinctly when he claimed that attitudes and behavior are shaped by the consequences of past actions. The power of that idea had been demonstrated by Ivan Pavlov and Skinner and others in experiments with dogs, pigeons, and other animals. Does this principle apply to human beings? In the sense that humans learn from experience, it does apply in general, but of course it does not tell us how people learn and what facilitates or blocks learning.

Individual piece-rate systems seemed to me an ideal test of *operant conditioning*. Like Pavlov's dogs and Skinner's pigeons, human beings learned that specific behavior could produce financial rewards, or, in psychological terms, reinforcements. Is that, in fact, what happens?

The weakness of the Skinner formulation can be demonstrated by examining the problems inherent in individual piece-rate incentives in industry. I have pointed out the following four types of problems (Whyte, 1972). Either I or one of my associates have found examples of each type of problem in our own fieldwork.

1. The Cost-Benefit Ratio and the Social Comparison Process. The laboratory experimenters could disregard the costs of the action to the actor because they were trifling, compared to the potential rewards. That is generally not the case in human affairs, where the important rewards we seek require substantial effort.

Other things being equal, most people rather would have more money than less and will make some effort to get more. The important question is: how much effort in relation to how much more money?

The answer to that question involves the rate-setting process—which is far from an exact science. When we were studying piece-rates years ago, we found many workers telling us that, with an all-out effort, they could earn some bonus money but too little to justify the effort. In that case, they would react in ways to penalize management. They would restrict production to well below the figure at which point they would begin to get the bonus, just getting the basic hourly rate guaranteed as long as the worker is on that job. Such a slow-down could spread readily to all workers affected by that rate. They would get the union to press a grievance, claiming that the incentive rate was "too tight" and urging management to order a new time-and-motion study and set a "looser rate."

What is equitable to a worker depends in part upon a social comparison process. Sometimes workers on a higher hourly base rate pay would find that others with lower hourly rates were earning more money because their particular jobs had a much "looser" piece rate. And then the workers on that lower job did not want to be "promoted" to a job where they would earn less money. The social comparison process also affects maintenance workers, who are not on piece rates because their output cannot be measured. Since they are more highly skilled than the piece-rate workers, when they find that the piece rates bring those less skilled people above them in earnings, they press the union to remedy this inequity by boosting their hourly pay.

2. Conflicting Stimuli. In a case described to me by Robert Kahn, a company had both an incentive system and a suggestion system. The individual, who wrote up a suggestion that was implemented by management, received a money award. On the other hand, if the suggestion involved changes in job methods, that gave management the right to make a new time-and-motion study on the job and to set a new rate, so that workers on that job would have to produce more to get the same incentive pay as before.

In many cases, individual workers devise improved working methods, that they then share with other workers but try to keep secret from the time-study man. If he discovered the invention, he would have the right to restudy the job. A new rate would be set, and all the workers would lose the gains made possible by an inventive worker. If one of those workers revealed their secret in writing up a suggestion, then he would gain—but at the expense of his fellow workers.

3. Time Lag and Trust. With pigeons and dogs, the time between the stimulus and the reinforcement is only a few seconds. With humans, few of a person's acts produce immediate rewards. The time lag between behavior and reinforcement is often days, weeks, or months.

Time lag involves the problem of the predictability of the behavior of those who control the administration of rewards and penalties. The question comes down to *trust*: Can I trust those administering the incentive system and the managers who have power over them?

The trust question depends on management's commitment not to change an incentive rate unless there has been a "major" or "substantial" change in methods, tools, or equipment used on a job. Between workers and management, we have found frequent disagreements as to what constitutes a "major" change. Furthermore, a series of minor changes over a period of months could well add up to a major change, but at what point does management intervene to change the rate? If workers have discovered a new and improved method to do the job, does management have the right to change the rate?

It is not my purpose to propose the *right* way to answer such questions. Management's answers have a major influence on the level of trust accorded management by the workers. This affects management's ability to gain the voluntary compliance of workers to its orders and suggestions.

4. The One-Body Problem. In the experiments of Pavlov or Skinner, we are interested only in the environmental conditions that induce the dog or the pigeon to behave in a certain way. We are not concerned with the motivation or behavior of Pavlov or Skinner.

When we apply *operant conditioning* to humans, we are no longer dealing with a one-body problem. Most of the rewards or penalties we experience are produced for us by other humans. We therefore need to examine the positive and negative reinforcements received by each party in the interpersonal or intergroup relationship.

Applying this conclusion to the economic incentive problem in industry makes it clear that we need to consider the costs and benefits management receives from individual piece-rate systems. When we were studying such systems in the 1950s, management people in general believed that piece-rate systems increased worker output, but many of them were wondering whether the gains achieved were worth the costs involved in operating the system. In the first place, these involved the salaries and fringe benefits and office space for time-and-motion study men, who established the rates. Furthermore, this was not a one-time cost for each job; every time there was thought to be a major change in equipment and job methods, a new study had to be made. The more rapidly technologies and job methods changed, the heavier the burden on management. In companies where technological and methods changes were especially frequent, it would become impractical to maintain a piece-rate system.

In some cases, most of the union grievances arose out of disputes on the incentive rates. Furthermore, those disputes seemed to be especially bitter. Workers would tell us about how management cheated them years ago in setting an incentive rate. Any manager concerned about maintaining good relations with workers and the union would have to be worried over the morale costs engendered by the piece-rate system.

A piece-rate system places a premium on productivity. Adequate quality is supposed to be assured by having a corps of inspectors checking on the performance of workers. That system has been losing favor among management people in recent years. Foreign competition has driven management to place a higher premium on quality. In many companies that has meant giving workers the responsibility to carry out quality checks on their output, thus eliminating most of the management quality inspectors. With the extra responsibility for checking quality, workers are under less pressure to increase output.

Management policies and practices have also shifted away from concentration on top-down pressure for production toward an increasing emphasis on a smooth flow of production among all of the departments producing components for the final product. Formerly companies tried to treat each department as if it were an independent unit, providing it with buffer stocks to work on at all times. Now the philosophy has shifted to recognize the waste involved in maintaining such stock piles and in moving them in and out of temporary storage areas. This has led to a "just-in-time" inventory and production system, involving a flow of parts and materials into a department just at the point when they are needed.

The new level of coordination and integration of departments now required cannot be achieved by foremen and other supervisors. If the new system is to work, workers must assume responsibility for minute to minute decisions. Management planners have come to recognize that their Japanese competitors operated with far fewer supervisory personnel for a given number of production workers, and this also has moved American managers to depend more heavily on worker skill and dedication.

The old system relied on motivating individual workers. The new system in many plants shifts the emphasis toward the development of work teams. The combination of all of these changes has served to make individual piece rates an anachronism.

We now recognize that individual incentives can motivate some workers to raise their production—within limits that are set by the physical and mental abilities of those workers but also by their fear of the consequences of producing as much as they can. The system was not designed for individuals but for all workers on those particular jobs. When we examine how the system is applied, we see that the positive aspects of piece rates can be outweighed by their negative effects on the social system and even by their negative economic impacts.

This sort of analysis indicates that a much broader theoretical framework would be required to deal effectively with the problems of motivation in industry. That would mean viewing the individual in the context of the group and the larger organization, which we will do in Chapter 7.

In exploring the limitations of the *operant conditioning* theory, we have already found ourselves dealing with economic variables. Now let us shift to a more direct focus on economics.

Economics was built on the assumption that human beings assess the potential costs and benefits of economic decisions and base their actions, as far as they are able, on what appears to be the most cost-effective thing to do. In his important book, *The Moral Dimension* (1988), Amitai Etzioni argues that humans also respond to their beliefs in what is the right thing to do, which often overrules what a strict economic calculus would dictate.

Let us assume that, if moral considerations did not stand in the way, humans would want to choose the most cost effective alternative. That leaves an important field for economics, and yet we still find serious problems in applying economic analysis to practical problems.

Economics arose out of a study of markets where individuals and organizations are actively engaged in buying and selling, and where some of the main costs and benefits are immediately observable. In organizations and communities, few economic incentives or disincentives have as immediate and direct effects as they do in the market. They have to be interpreted in a social and organizational structural context.

An undergraduate degree with a major in economics hardly qualifies me as an economist, yet I find nevertheless that my own research interests have led me to focus on economic factors—and then to find economic problems that few professional economists have dealt with effectively.

I found such problems in industry when studying the transformation of the Xerox Corporation and reading up on the mania for corporate buyouts and other changes in ownership and control in the 1980s. I also found such problems in rural and community development in Peru.

Studies in industry led me to point out two important limitations in current methods of economic analysis, (a) failure to deal with the symbolic means of measuring money flows, and (b) failure to distinguish the interests of the key decision maker from those of his firm.

In the large industrial firm, money flows are not observed and measured directly; they are represented symbolically by *industrial accounting*. I never had studied accounting; I had simply assumed that the figures presented in company financial reports and profit and loss statements represented firm realities—unless some people were manipulating the books. In the course of a study of the ways that Xerox Corporation restructured itself to compete effectively with other national and international firms, we encountered arguments between workers and their union about methods of measuring labor costs.

Anyone proposing to study economic decision making in such a firm would not measure and trace the money itself. He/she would focus on how the decision maker would interpret the accounting figures. If one wished to go behind those accounting figures, he/she would find that the systems and formulas are based upon certain conventional assumptions, which may—or may not—reflect adequately the economic performance of the firm.

This is well illustrated with the problem of allocating indirect or overhead costs in relation to direct labor costs (the costs of labor, including fringe benefit costs for those directly producing the product). It had become common practice to allocate indirect costs in relation to direct labor costs. In the early years of mass production, direct labor represented a very large proportion of total costs, so the proportional allocation of indirect costs to direct labor costs had no serious distorting effects. Today, when direct labor costs range between 5 and 15 percent of total costs, the distorting effects of such an accounting formula have serious economic and human consequences.

As I read up on the recent research literature on industrial accounting, I encountered the following case (Hayes et al., 1988).

We know of one high-tech company whose overhead costs add up to almost ten times its direct labor costs, which come to roughly ten dollars per hour. Managers in this company are motivated to buy a part from an outside vendor, if at all possible, instead of making it internally because in so doing they reduce the costs for which they are responsible (which include the allocated costs) by $(1+10) \times \$10$, or $110, for each direct labor hour saved. Managing an increasing volume of subcontracting, however, requires additional overhead personnel. Therefore, this company finds that its direct labor costs are decreasing, while its overhead costs are increasing—which drives up its overhead allocation rate for the remaining products and motivates its managers to subcontract even more. While extreme, this company is not atypical of many today that are being driven in unanticipated directions by the apparently innocuous mandates of their accounting systems.

This suggests that the "hollowing out" of the American corporation has not occurred simply in response to inexorable economic and technological forces, but is driven in part by the supposedly rational application of accounting conventions. Following the conventional logic of accounting leads to irrational outcomes from the standpoint of those concerned with maintaining employment and the economic health of American manufacturing.

In legal theory and in our courts, the corporation is treated as if it were an individual. Economists seem to reason regarding the economic welfare of the firm on the basis of accepting a legal fiction as if it were a fact.

Decision-makers argue that their decisions are shaped solely by their concern for the economic welfare of the firm. The chief executive officer (CEO) who persuades his board of directors to provide him with millions of dollars deferred compensation, in case of a hostile takeover, will argue that such financial security enables him to perform better for the company, but do we really believe that is what motivates him?

Consider also the practice of "taking the company private." A group within top management arranges to borrow enormous sums from a bank to finance the purchase of the company's stock and thus take it off the market. Since the price paid may be 50 to 100 percent higher than the current market price, the private company emerges from the transaction with an enormous debt load, which may have negative consequences on its future performance. Nevertheless, unless the company later goes bankrupt, the organizers of the transactions are likely to gain large financial benefits. It may be more to their advantage to hold large pieces of a struggling company than to hold much smaller pieces of a more profitable company.

In many large companies, bankers serve on the boards of directors. Are economic decisions dictated or influenced by banking interests?

The actions of key decision-makers can also be strongly influenced by personal networks outside of the company. The collapse of the Prado economic/political/social empire in Peru in the 1970s provides vivid examples of such phenomena. For more than a century, the Prado family had held predominant positions in those three interrelated fields of human activity. In the 1940s, Manuel Prado had been president, and he was president once more from 1956 to 1962. His younger brother, Mariano Prado, had been president and CEO of the Banco Popular, one of Peru's largest banks, which also had strong links to many industrial companies owned by members of the family or close friends.

After the collapse of the Banco Popular, which brought down many companies associated with it, the investigation launched by President Fernando Belaunde Terry (who had been for years a strong critic of the Prados) revealed a striking tale of mismanagement. Furthermore, this was not simply mismanagement by inefficient employees. The mismanagement was systematically directed toward the support of the Prado family and close friends and political and military allies. To understand the rise and fall of the Banco Popular, it would be pure folly to regard it as an individual person, who was guided by judgment of what contributed to the economic prosperity of the business enterprise. To be sure, the Banco Popular case may be regarded as extreme and not truly representative of how corporations are usually governed. In a highly developed industrial state, there will be legal controls that limit some of the "abuses" described in that case, yet the analyst will need to consider the networks of individuals, groups, and organizations outside the firm which can influence the actions of key decision makers in the firm.

For economists to go beyond the world of legal fiction and deal with realities in the economics of the firm, we need intensive studies of actual cases in which key decision makers are making decisions ostensibly in the interests of the firm but also involving their personal interests—and responding to social and political interests outside of the firm.

Now let us switch the economic focus to agricultural research and development, focusing particularly on our studies of the economic responses of small farmers in Peru. Here we are not only concerned with the immediate costs and benefits farmers and their families receive from farming, but also with the physical infrastructure and the community social organization that influences farmer responses to economic factors (Whyte & Williams, 1968; Whyte, 1991).

We presented a typology of four types of situations involving improvement projects that might be introduced by change agents.

1. Individual Direct. Here the payoff is to the individual or his family in direct relationship to the investment in labor and materials by that unit. Such would be the case on the farm when the individual family tries a new seed, invests in fertilizer, applies insecticide, and so on.

2. Individual Through Group with Equitable Sharing. Here the individual and his family receives the rewards from completion of a project in which he has participated as a member of a group. In many villages, the small farmers have organized themselves to build public improvements such as a reservoir to provide potable water, to bring in electricity, or to build or improve a road.

We should note that such projects can be different from one another in the sanctions that can be exercised against those who did not work on the project. Families that did not participate can be prevented from installing pipes in their homes to bring in the potable water or can be denied home connections to the electric power supply. Even if the government did not intervene locally, it would not be practical for the villagers to police the road so that it was only used by families who had worked on the project. In other words, "free riders" can be readily dealt with in some projects, but in others compliance depends on local leadership and the strength of the community organization—topics we will explore further in dealing with social organization.

3. The Differential Impact Project. Some members of the community stand to gain much more than others or some members may gain while others lose. In communities where some families own far more farm land than others, reducing that discrepancy necessarily involves extracting some resources from the wealthier citizens. For example, in one case, the community carried out a large reforestation project. In a government sponsored program, the seedlings were supplied and people were paid for planting them. Everybody who worked on the project was rewarded, but the families who owned large herds of cattle lost through the elimination of some of their grazing land. Such projects present problems in leadership and community organization.

4. Controlling Individual Interests in Favor of Group Interests. If the community as a whole is to benefit, individual members must be restrained from doing what would be rewarding only to them and their families. This represents what the economists call the tragedy of the *commons*.

Such cases often are found in the field of animal husbandry, where the village faces a problem of overgrazing. If there were no limits on the number of cattle each family has on the range, the cattle would eat the grass to the roots and turn the range into a desert. That danger may be clear to everybody, but if one family clandestinely allows more than its share of cattle on the range, that family profits from the sacrifices exacted on all the others.

In all four types of cases, economic incentives are involved, and yet the problems of organizing and carrying out improvement projects are quite different in each case.

In type 1 (*Individual Direct*) the organizational problem is relatively simple. If the proposed improvement in farming methods can be demonstrated to be practical and affordable by the farm family, the farmer can make the change without being concerned with what his neighbors do. For the change agent, it will be more efficient to discuss the proposed improvement with village leaders in order to reach a large number of potential adopters, but the project can be implemented if only one or a few families adopt it at the outset. If those few adopters get good results from the innovation with their first crop, others in the community will observe their results and talk with the adopters about their experiences.

In that case, the innovation becomes a self-propelling project. In fact, this can happen even without the intervention of a change agent. What was at one time one of the most widely used potato varieties developed by the International Potato Center in Peru began to spread among small farmers even before it was officially released by the Center. The experimental plots were protected by wire barriers, but outsiders could get close enough to observe plant growth that looked promising. Some farmers got into the enclosure, pulled out several plants, and planted them in their own fields. When the new variety did well, farmers shared plants with relatives. Through informal processes of observation and exchange of information, the innovation spread rapidly.

Up to the 1950s, many social scientists believed that peasant farmers were so locked into their traditional culture that they resisted change, and that therefore the problem was to discover methods to overcome this resistance to change. We are now calling this "the myth of the passive peasant." In our studies in Peru and elsewhere in Latin America, we find that although small farmers are reluctant to try an innovation that entails a large risk, they are quick to try out something new on a small scale. If that works out, the next year they can devote more of their land to the new variety or new crop. When they reject an innovation, it is generally because they can't afford the expense entailed or because their experience with their particular plot indicates correctly that it is not practical under their conditions.

For type 2, *Individual Through Group with Equitable Sharing*, the problem is more complex. Such a project involves community organization and leadership. It also involves a level of trust among the members and between members and leaders. People have to believe that others will do their fair share and that they personally will benefit from the hoped for rewards. If the project allows for the presence of "free riders," they will want to know that something will be done to make them participate. Local history will also be an important influence. If the community has worked well together on successful improvement projects, this improves the chances of community acceptance of and participation in the new project. If there has been no previous experience with improvement projects, it will be more difficult to secure acceptance and participation. And, if the community has had experiences with projects that failed, amid mutual recriminations, it may be especially difficult to mobiliize people for a new project.

Type 3, *The Differential Impact Project*, presents a still more complex organizational problem because the potential divisions within the community are based on structural and economic differences in resources. If a large majority of the families would benefit from the project, it may be possible to mobilize them to put some money and effort into it, but the leaders must expect to encounter an entrenched opposition. Then the problem becomes one of overcoming the opposition or working out with them some side deal in which they get something for what they are giving up.

Type 4, *Controlling Individual Interests in Favor of Group Interests*, adds a new dimension of problems: devising and implementing a system of policing and enforcement. The community would have to organize volunteers or hire someone to see to it that everybody abides by the rules decided upon. In the case of the cattle overgrazing problem, that would require watchmen and also a system of branding cattle so that those policing could keep track of how many cattle each family had on the range. These problems may be too difficult for the community to handle by itself, and the villagers would need the intervention of government or some private agency outside of the community. In the case of the cattle problem, the outside agency could help to organize the local policing problem and could offer further incentives for compliance. If many people are required to give up some of their cattle, they could be compensated by being helped to acquire cattle that are healthier than their current stock and that make better use of the grazing land.

In all of the cases we have examined, there was no question that economic incentives did have impacts on behavior, but understanding those impacts depends on the social and economic context within which the incentives operate. We also have to answer a number of questions. How do individuals measure the costs and benefits? Who makes the determination regarding how the costs and benefits should be distributed? How has the system been organized and how have individual actors responded to it in the past?

What does this discussion of the psychological and economic aspects of incentives add up to? When I was writing this, from the early 1950s to the 1980s, it represented a novel approach to the study of human motivation: rethinking the human responses to piece rates and the economic analysis of the responses in industry, business, and agriculture. Our discovery of what we call "the myth of the passive peasant" indicated that many researchers were wasting enormous amounts of time and money studying how to overcome peasant resistance to change. Our studies indicated that the problems were not cultural but technical, economic, and organizational.

Note that our critiques were not the products of armchair theorizing but rather arose in response to confronting problem situations in the field. What was my personal intellectual contribution? That is impossible to determine, since these findings arose out of collaborative research with students and colleagues at Chicago and Cornell and at the Instituto de Estudios Peruanos for our rural research. I found I was getting nearly as much satisfaction from the ideas generated by my collaborators as I did from my own ideas.

In all of the cases analyzed here, success in achieving economic gains depended to a small or to an enormous extent on *organization*. We now turn to the *organization* problem, to see if we can link it with socio-economics.

CHAPTER SEVEN

SOCIO-TECHNICAL SYSTEMS

Within a work organization, what is the relationship between social relations and the technological or technical organization? My fieldwork led me toward the answer to that question, yet I failed to see what I had done. It took Eric Trist's formulation of the *socio-technical systems* framework to jolt me onto a new theoretical and fieldwork track.

When I began my studies of industry in the 1940s, I was guided by Burleigh Gardner's principle that "the factory is a social system." When I read "Some Social and Psychological Consequences of the Longwall Method of Coal Getting" (Trist & Bamforth, 1951), I realized this was an important article, but at first I did not know how to integrate it into my theorizing. It took me several years to see the significance of Eric Trist's creation of the *socio-technical* framework, which set in motion a basic reorientation of theory and practice in organizational studies.

The concept is simple, but it has enormous theoretical and practical implications. As I see it, this tells us that the factory (or any work organization) is not only a social system but also a technical system, consisting of the technologies and tools and work procedures required to meet the organization's objectives. This means that the social and the technical systems are mutually dependent: a change in the technical system necessarily impacts on the functioning of the social system, and a change in the social system has impacts on the technical system.

Two years before the Trist breakthrough, I published one of my better articles, under the title of "The Social Structure of the Restaurant"(1949). In hindsight, I should have called it "The Socio-Technical Structure of the

Restaurant" because that was what I was describing and analyzing—without recognizing that what I was doing required this more inclusive theoretical framework.

A restaurant is a combination of a production and a service organization. Coordination of those two activities is a simple matter in a diner or small restaurant. The larger the firm becomes, the more difficult the coordination task becomes. This is especially true if the large restaurant operates on two or more floors.

In Stouffer's Restaurant in Chicago's Loop District, where I concentrated my own fieldwork, the kitchen was in the basement and food was served on the upper two floors. In the noon rush hour, customers came in and were seated and served and charged at the cashier's station on the way out, all within little over half an hour.

With the exception of the manager, the employees were all women. Dieticians worked with the cooks, keeping them to the standard recipes of the Stouffer chain. Food trays were lifted mechanically to the two service pantries on the upper floors.

Pantry supervisors had the responsibility of ordering resupplies from the kitchen. They communicated their orders primarily through the teleautograph, where the written order there showed up also in the kitchen. If the communication seemed urgent, the supervisor could use the house telephone, but that call would tie up all the phones in the restaurant, blocking off any other calls from anywhere in the restaurant, so employees were urged to use it vary sparingly.

The third medium of communication from kitchen to service floors was face-to-face communication. During the noon rush hour, I sometimes observed dieticians running upstairs to observe and talk with pantry supervisors. The dieticians claimed that the service pantry people would get panicky and place orders for much more than was needed. In that case, when the rush hour was over, the firm would be left with a large volume of left-overs. The dieticians had the responsibility of meeting consumer demand and keeping left-overs to a minimum.

Waitresses took the customers' orders to the service pantry and called them in there. When several waitresses came in at about the same time, I sometimes observed frictions among them and with service pantry personnel.

In another large and busy restaurant, the waitresses were served by pantry men. This seemed to make for greater friction, as the men were not accustomed to taking orders from women. Sometimes, to relieve the pressures on them, they would just step back from the counter and leave the waitresses waiting and fuming.

There seemed to be two ways of minimizing this friction, interpersonally and technologically. Edith Lentz observed one counterman's system when two or more waitresses came to him at about the same time. Before filling any order, he would glance over all the orders and fill the ones that were similar first and then go on to the others. This meant that the waitress who came in first was not necessarily the first one to be served, but still the system was so fast and efficient that no one was kept waiting long.

The technological solution was the *spindle*, a spike on a stand. As she came in, each waitress placed her order on the spike, which provided an automatically queuing system so there could be no quarrel over who got there first. (Some people have given me credit for inventing this important piece of technology. In fact, it was my research assistant, Edith Lentz, who discovered it as it was installed in one restaurant she studied.)

Waitress work is generally thought of as a low-skilled occupation. In a large and busy restaurant, it seemed to me that the job required a high degree of *social* skill. When the hostess seated the customers on her station, the waitress would immediately come by, give the customers menus, and tell them that she would be back shortly to take their orders. That avoided the situation when the customer got restless, called out, or clinked a glass to get attention. The skillful waitress did not just respond to the customer but took the initiative to tell him or her what seemed to be especially good today—guiding them to items she could get without delay. She was well aware of the situation in the service pantry, so she would tell the customer when a particular order might take 10 or 15 minutes to deliver. If the customer stuck to his original order, he would not get upset by waiting.

In essence, the skillful waitress did not simply respond to the customer. She took the initiative in guiding his or her orders and thus influenced the work flow in the kitchen and service pantries.

Years later, I sent a reprint of my article to Eric Trist, suggesting that mine was a socio-technical analysis. He agreed. Of course, I did not claim priority for this socio-technical analysis because I did not recognize the significance of what I had done. If you want your contribution to be recognized, in the first place you have to recognize it yourself and give it a label so that others can recognize it and integrate it into their own thinking.

My restaurant article was reprinted widely, so my colleagues recognized that I had done something interesting. In retrospect, I look back on that article as a lost opportunity, not simply to claim credit but, more importantly, to focus my fieldwork and analysis on the socio-technical systems much sooner than I did.

At the practical level, the socio-technical framework tells us that those planning to introduce new technologies should at the same time study and try to anticipate the ways this change will impact upon the social system. They should also focus on ways that the social system can be modified to fit with the technical system and on ways that aspects of the technical system can be modified to fit with the social system.

This is an important message. In the past, it was customary for planners of the introduction of new technologies to concentrate on working out the engineering aspects of the change. The engineers designed the technical system in all its details, and then turned the problems of determining what new jobs had to be created and how those new jobs should be fitted into the social system to those responsible for human resources planning. Such nonintegrative planning nearly always led to disturbances in the social system, and those disturbances often prevented the innovation from yielding the economic benefits the engineers had predicted for it.

Where do *socio-technical systems* fit into the theorizing of mainstream sociologists studying organizational behavior? The answer to that question appears to be *nowhere*.

One of the frameworks discussed by Richard Hall (1991), the rational contingency model does seem to lay the groundwork for socio-technical thinking. It does so by challenging the old scientific management principle that there is a one best way to structure an industrial or business organization. Studying firms in different lines of industry and business, Paul Lawrence and Jay Lorsch (1967) found that firms in each line tended to organize themselves in ways that were different from patterns prevailing in other types of firms. They argued that these differences were not deviations from some imagined norm but rather necessary adaptations to the various lines of business being developed.

The *socio-technical systems* model recognizes different patterns of overall organization, according to the line of industrial or business activity, but goes beyond this generalization to point out that, even in firms pursuing the same line of business, there are many options in the tools and technologies that can be used and also many options regarding the way the social system is developed to utilize the tools and technologies.

In his popular textbook, Hall (1991) does not mention Eric Trist as an important organizational behavior theorist. In fact, Trist appears in that book in just one footnote that has nothing to do with *socio-technical systems*. Hall concentrates his theoretical attention on sociologists that presented frameworks to explain aspects of bureaucratic organizations. A recent book by English organizational sociologists (Morgan & Stanley, 1993) indicates that English sociologists are also still stuck with the unproductive effort to create an organizational theory that would fit all bureaucratic organizations under all conditions.

If you ask a mainstream organizational sociologist to explain the basic characteristics of bureaucracies, he won't recognize that that is a silly question. He or she should want to know, are you talking about bureaucracies in private industry or in not-for-profit agencies? Are you concerned with manufacturing organizations, continuous process organizations (such as petroleum refineries), commercial organizations (department stores, hotels, restaurants), governmental agencies, and so on? Unless the researcher focuses the bureaucracy question in terms of these and many other questions relating to the specific organization being studied, there is no hope of scientific or practical progress.

How can we explain the failure of mainstream sociologists to recognize the importance of Trist's conception of socio-technical systems? Was it because Trist was a social psychologist, whose doctorate was in psychology? That seems unlikely because sociologists recognize their close links with psychology through social psychology, a subfield both disciplines share. Was it because Trist was an Englishman who developed his ideas on socio-technical systems while working with the Tavistock Institute of Human Relations in London? That also seems unlikely because Tavistock was well known to American sociologists and Trist spent the years after 1960 working with the Wharton School of the University of Pennsylvania, York University in Canada, and other universities in this hemisphere. Furthermore, that would not account for the neglect of Trist among mainstream English sociologists.

I find the answer to that question through distinguishing between "pure" (mainstream) sociologists and those doing applied work in organizational behavior. The applied sociologists, like other behavioral scientists working in industry, necessarily use a socio-technical strategy or some modification of it, as for example in the framework proposed by Neil Tichy (1983), in which he divides what Trist calls "social" into "political" and "cultural" elements. We use it because in consulting with plant managers and other executives regarding the introduction of social and structural changes we necessarily have to work with them to consider how such changes will affect the technical system and how changes in the technical system will affect the social system.

Mainstream sociologists are under no such pressures to advance from theory to practice. They can build and maintain their scholarly reputations by joining in academic debates about global frameworks underlying the growth and survival of bureaucratic organizations.

CHAPTER EIGHT

STUDYING CULTURES AND INTERCULTURAL RELATIONS

S tudying cultures and intercultural relations was for me a long-term and complicated agenda. In order to remain involved in the fieldwork I needed to organize a research program in new ways that I had to discover.

That was not a one-person job. I would need to work with others and their organizations. Financial support would help me to hire research assistants, but money would not buy dedicated collaborators. I would have to find ways of offering potential collaborators ways of serving their own interests as well as mine.

In my work in Peru, beginning in 1961, I had my most far reaching and extended experience with combining *Joint-Payoffs* with *Multi-Objective* planning.

My first experience in Latin America was in my sabbatical year, 1954–55. In a research project supported by Creole Petroleum Company (a subsidiary of what became Exxon), I was studying the relations between Venezuelan personnel and expatriate American managers. Through that experience, I was learning to speak Spanish and to begin to fit into Latin American cultural patterns. Still, on problems between U.S. managers and Venezuelan workers and *capetazes* (subforemen), I could not disentangle the organizational structural effects from the intercultural problems. For my next Latin American project, I needed to go to a country where I would be studying the relations between Latin American managers and Latin American workers and supervisors.

On my sabbatical (1961–62) I chose Peru. Cornell social anthropologist Allan R. Holmberg introduced me to that country through his applied project at Vicos, which involved transforming a hacienda operated by mestizos into a self governing indigenous community. That seemed to me the most exciting project going on at that time, and I welcomed the chance to be introduced to Peru through Allan, who had built up strong ties with eminent Peruvians through the Vicos Project—even though at that time I had no thought of doing rural studies in Peru.

I got support for that sabbatical from a Fullbright Fellowship and a grant from the National Institute for Mental Health for a study of "The Human Problems of Industrial Development in Peru." In the early months of our year in Peru, I became aware of a phenomenon which upset my assumption that I would be studying industrial relations among those immersed in Peruvian culture. I found that Peruvian industrial development had been based largely on foreign ownership. There were indeed Peruvian entrepreneurs, who had built substantial companies but, with very few exceptions, they were all either immigrants (mainly from Europe) or sons of immigrants.

This led me to assume that Peruvian culture was unfriendly toward industrial entrepreneurship. To understand such a phenomenon, I set out to immerse myself in Peruvian culture.

How could I accomplish such an immersion? I read up on Peruvian history in general but concentrated on children's history books, to discover what role models were offered to the young people. I read the newspapers, concentrating on the reporting of business news. I read *Caretas*, Peru's most popular news and discussion magazine.

I found no industrial entrepreneurs as role models for Peruvian children. The heroes were military leaders who had lost their lives in Peru's disastrous war against Chile. When his troops were surrounded by superior Chilean forces, with no possibility of escape or resupply, General Benavidas called his officers together and told them, in effect, "You are young and have a future to look forward to. You are free to surrender. But I am old. I will fight here until I have shot my last cartridge." The troops then followed him and continued to fight until their ammunition was exhausted.

General Alfonso Ugarte was leading his cavalry in a battle on a cliff hanging over the Pacific Ocean, when he saw the soldier carrying the

Peruvian flag being struck down. To save the flag from being trampled under Chilean feet, the General spurred his horse forward, grabbed the flag and held it high as he and his horse plunged off the cliff to their deaths. His statue, mounted appropriately on his horse, is displayed in a prominent intersection in Lima.

Admiral Miguel Grau commanded his ship when it was overwhelmed by the superior Chilean fleet. Rather than surrender, he went down with his ship.

These men had not *achieved* anything, but were celebrated for their courage and patriotism. The one exception among role model heroes was Jorge Chavez, who was the first man to fly over the Alps, but his achievement was somewhat ambiguous, since he lost his life when his plane crashed upon landing.

I found the Peruvians had trouble in expressing words for *achievement* or its synonym, *accomplishment*, in English. By those words we mean gaining an important result through persistent and dedicated effort. The Peruvian problem may be rooted in the Spanish language, which has several words for a successful result that do not distinguish whether it has been arrived at with one's own efforts or through good luck or personal connections.

The newspapers ran stories of strictly business news of the firms of the Peruvian entrepreneurs, but I never saw any accounts of the "rags to riches" tales familiar to me in my own country. As my research assistant, Graciela Flores explained to me, the children and grandchildren of the entrepreneur did not want to be reminded publicly that their families had not always been prominent socially as well as industrially.

How does one study the culture of a country—while simultaneously carrying on field studies of industrial relations? I remembered that, in the 1950s, some of my colleagues in Cornell's Department of Sociology and Anthropology had done a study of the values of students in various American colleges. A leader of that study, Rose Goldsen sent me the questionnaire they had used along with some discussion of their results. I worked with Graciela Flores to adapt that questionnaire to the Peruvian situation, discarding some items, and adding others specifically designed for Peru.

We included items on choices of careers, but Peruvian students had chosen their desired careers upon entering the university, so we decided to apply the survey to public and private high school seniors. To gain access to those schools, I called on the Director of the Instituto Psicopedagogico Nacional in the Ministry of Education to suggest that our survey be jointly sponsored by Cornell and his Instituto. He had a very small staff and no funds for research, so was delighted with the arrangement.

Graciela and I worked with the Director to select the public schools and three status level of private schools in Lima. To schedule the appointments for each school, the Director telephoned the school principal. The most reluctant principal said it would be better to apply the survey at 10 o'clock rather than the 9 o'clock that we had planned—and we were glad to comply.

This procedure made it possible for Graciela to survey 12 Lima schools within a three-week period. (In the U.S. carrying out such an extensive survey would have taken many months to work out arrangements with school boards, superintendents, principals, etc.) While I did not approve of this way of doing things, I was glad to have a powerful educational bureaucracy working for us. When the men on our staff went to several provincial cities for their industrial studies, they were armed with a letter from the Instituto Director telling local school authorities to cooperate with us. We had not planned to do any studies in Equities in the jungle, but when the Instituto Director went there on Ministry business, he took our surveys to the high school there.

We were overwhelmed with these data, but, with Rose Goldsen working with Graciela and me primarily on the Lima data, we got a rich harvest to report (Whyte, 1963). More than ever before, I was appreciating the values of survey research.

By now I was captured by the lure of Peru and ready to commit myself for longer-term studies. I had learned about the Career Achievement Awards from N.I.M.H. that would provide the ILR School of $25,000 to cover my salary providing I committed myself to focus on research, to the exclusion of all administrative activities, for five years, with the possibility of renewals for other periods up to my 65th birthday, when I planned to retire.

Allan Holmberg and I got together on a research plan to write a book on the culture and industrial and rural development of Peru. He would study rural changes and development, I would study industrial relations, and we would get together on studies of Peruvian culture.

That plan was aborted when Allan came down with leukemia and shortly died. I assumed that I would continue with my industrial studies with my assistants. In order to make contacts with industrial management, I got myself invited to a luncheon meeting of The Friends and Members of IPAE, the Peruvian management association. Over drinks before lunch, Interim Director of IPAE, Robert R. Braun got me aside to talk about my research plans. After graduating from high school in Austria, he had come to Peru. After several industrial jobs in German, American, and Peruvian firms, he had set himself up as a management consultant along with his half-time job with IPAE.

After hearing me out, he expressed strong interest in my industrial studies and volunteered to help me present my plans to management people and help me to gain access to their firms. I did call on him and found that he meant everything he said. Shortly we became partners in my studies, with Bob Braun guiding me and critiqueing my presentations to management people.

What did Bob Braun get out of his collaboration with me? We found that we enjoyed working together. We published one article together, "On Language and Culture" (1968), and my talk at an IPAE meeting on the results of my studies went over very well, so he could take credit for that as my informal sponsor. (Later, I wrote a strong letter of recommendation for Bob to become CEO of the International Association of Scientific Management. He got the job and moved to Switzerland.)

I had not planned to do any surveys in industry, but Bob tried to talk me into a broad survey program. I resisted but then I compromised with him, agreeing to carry out one survey in Empresas Electricas (Lima Light and Power Company). I chose that firm because I knew that Lawrence K. Williams, now with ILR in Cornell, had been study director of a survey of Detroit Edison when he was at the University of Michigan. I wrote Larry to invite him to collaborate with me on a comparative study of the two electrical power companies. Thus began my partnership with Larry that lasted many years, through industrial studies and then into rural research.

I had assumed that Allan's death had closed the door on my Peruvian rural studies, but now two events propelled me into that field. John Hickman, who had been a graduate student with Allan, was then doing field studies of indigenous communities in the Lake Titicaca high plains region of Peru. He had heard about our high school values surveys and asked me if he could use some of our items. I had no idea which ones to suggest, but he went ahead anyway, taking some of our items, adding some of his own, and getting them translated into the indigenous languages of

Quechua and Aymara. He was happy with his results, which encouraged me to believe it could be interesting and useful to develop this line of research in Peru.

The second propelling event was the election of Fernando Belaunde Terry as President of Peru in 1963. A former Dean of the College of Architecture, Belaunde had waged a strenuous campaign throughout the country, going even into remote rural areas, to stress one of his main planks: land reform and participative rural development. He brought in with him a group of men dedicated to his reform program and eager to get started.

If Belaunde's rural reform program was about to set in motion large changes in rural villages, would it not be important to carry out baseline studies on a number of villages during 1994, the year the program would be starting and then do follow-up studies 5 years later to show the before-and-after measures of government induced changes?

I had in mind also combining intensive case studies along with the surveys in each community selected. Through Allan, I had met José Matos Mar, then known as Peru's leading anthropologist. He had been a consultant to Belaunde on rural development. When I talked over my plans with him, he responded enthusiastically. Furthermore, he told me that he had a group of students preparing to go to make anthropological studies of rural communities in the Chancay Valley, about 35 miles north of Lima on the coast. If I could be there at that time with a survey ready, with modest additional financial support for the students, we could do a pretest and then do surveys on four villages. He also invited me and Cornell to make our headquarters in Peru in the Instituto de Estudios Peruanos (IEP), which he directed. The IEP initially was financed by a government grant.

I returned to Cornell to discuss these new plans. I suggested a joint agreement between Cornell and IEP, with Larry and me being codirectors along with José Matos Mar. Larry responded enthusiastically. We worked together on the questionnaire, and I took it back to Peru in January 1964 to work with the students and Matos in the Chancay Valley.

With very limited funds, how could we get surveys made in a number of villages representing Peru's main regions? If we could work out collaborative arrangements with a professor of sociology or anthropology in several regional universities, we would have, along with the Chancay Valley study, a wide range of villages for our surveys and case studies. If the university could provide a vehicle to get its students in the field, I would work with the professors to train the students for the anthropological and survey operations. The collaborating university would have access to all the data collected by their students.

Following this research plan, we surveyed 26 villages in four regions of Peru throughout 1964. I now had got myself into the largest research program I had ever attempted. I had always regarded administrative work as a necessary evil. I realized now that, if we were going to be successful, I would have to rethink my views of administration so as to make it an *intellectual* challenge, something that was not only necessary but important as a new approach to theorizing about administrative leadership.

It was at that point that I saw the connection between *Joint-Payoff* transactions and *Multi-Objective* planning. In order to get and analyze our research data, we had to develop a strategy in which Peruvian professors and graduate students were full partners in the enterprise. I had heard talk in Peru about "academic imperialism" in which U.S. professors came in, hired Peruvian students to gather their data, and then took all the data home with them to write academic articles and gain academic advancement.

To avoid that patron-peon relationship, we needed to think what objectives the Peruvians working with us wanted to reach and then to plan accordingly. We agreed that our program should serve to strengthen the capacities for survey and anthropological research in the universities that were collaborating with us and particularly with the IEP, our home base in Peru. We agreed that we would encourage our Peruvian professors and students in our program to publish from their own research in Spanish—and, in the first few years, our group published more in Spanish than in English.

We planned to serve the interests of Cornell's Latin American Studies Program through our publications and through the teaching that Larry and I did on the basis of our program. For several years, Larry and I conducted research seminars based on our Peruvian surveys and anthropological studies. Giorgio Alberti came to us from Italy; while working for his doctoral degree in sociology and organizational behavior, he used our seminar to prepare himself for research in Peru. He did so well there that we hired him as a research associate to represent Cornell full time with the IEP.

Our multi-objective strategy worked so well that we were able to carry out our overall plans even when we were unable to achieve one or more of our objectives. Through an 11-year period, Cornell and IEP continued active collaboration in spite of the rising tensions between our two countries. The relationship ended only when we at Cornell went on to other activities.

————————————————————•◆•◆•————————————————————

What did we get out of this relationship—beyond something of a record in an enduring international research and teaching collaboration? Let me concentrate on what I personally learned.

I learned that my original rationale for planning the ambitious survey and anthropological research program was simply wrong. I had accepted the common academic rationale that peasants in villages tended to be locked into their traditional cultures; in order for change to take place, some outside forces were needed to "overcome the resistance to change."

I had assumed that Belaunde's rural reform program would provide those forces. Thus it was important to survey a number of villages before those outside forces had their impact and then resurvey them 5 years later to assess the changes that had taken place. The case studies would help us to explain the processes of change in the villages.

In fact, those Belaunde forces of rural change never manifested themselves. In congress, the president faced an opposition majority that blocked and sabotaged his major rural reform efforts.

Nevertheless, although my prediction failed to come off, that experience led us to an important theoretical conclusion. We found many of our villages changing in major ways through their own internal dynamics, without any governmental reform efforts. This discovery led me to write about "the myth of the passive peasants." I was learning that unless some external force controlled and exploited them—as in the case of mestizo authorities with the indigenous population—the peasants were able and willing to change their practices and beliefs, to try an agricultural innovation on a small scale, and then expand on it if it worked.

Beyond this revelation, we got a series of case studies of development and change, much of which is described in *Power, Politics, and Progress: Social Change in Rural Peru* (Whyte & Alberti, 1976). Methodologically, we learned a great deal about combining surveys with intensive case studies (see Chapter 9).

In cross-cultural studies, comparing Peruvian high school seniors with U.S. college students, Lima Sears Roebuck and Co. with a comparable U.S. store, and Empresas Electricas with Detroit Edison, we learned about different expectations regarding authority and also differences in the level of personal trust. At that time, Peruvians were not inclined to trust anybody outside of their families (Whyte, 1963; Whyte & Williams, 1963).

We also learned the value of collaboration in research operations. Without the very active collaboration we enjoyed, it would not have been possible to carry out such a large and long lasting research program.

CHAPTER NINE
ON COMBINING RESEARCH METHODS

C an we learn something from combining surveys with social anthropological field studies, that we could not learn if we did one or the other separately? That was the question we proposed to answer in our village study program.

By the time our Peruvian village program started, I already had fairly substantial experience with surveys, but only in situations where we had little qualitative interviewing to back them up. For the village studies, we saw our first opportunity to do intensive case studies in combination with surveys.

In 1964 our research team carried out surveys in 26 villages, but then we had to drop many of them for two main reasons. The political situation at the University of Arequipa and the University of Huamonga in Ayacucho made it impossible to continue the program to 1969 in their areas. Since the anthropological case studies took much longer field and writing time, many of our anthropological reports on some of the remaining villages were so inadequate that we had to drop them. We ended up with a sample of 12 villages in four regions of Peru where we believed we had solid data for both the 1964 and 1969 surveys along with good case studies.

I thought it important to try this combination of methods, but I had no idea of how they would fit together. I was delighted to find that they not only fitted, but also offered a significant contribution to social theory, which would not have been possible using either method alone.

That payoff came particularly through a study of perceived cooperation and conflict on community maintenance or improvement projects. In line with then current sociological thinking, I had perceived conflict and cooperation as opposite ends of the same continuum.

When I read the student's report on the village of Mito, I was surprised to find that he had found the village low in both cooperation and conflict in 1969. I asked myself, "How could that possibly be?" I then checked the survey responses of Mito on these items and found that they confirmed the anthropological report.

Was this a fluke, or was I on to something important? We had expected a high *negative* correlation between responses to these two items. Williams ran the correlations for both 1964 and 1969 surveys. In both cases, he found the correlations as close to zero as one could get without cooking the data.

We then abandoned our one-dimensional cooperation-conflict model in favor of a two-dimensional model, one dimension for high-to-low cooperation, another for high-to-low conflict. When we put those two dimensions perpendicular to each other, we got a four-box model, with the dividing lines placed at the average values for conflict and cooperation for all the 12 villages. We then placed each village according to its average score for each dimension for 1964 and again for 1969. For both years, we found villages that fell into each of the four boxes.

As Table 9.1 indicates, columns 1 and 2 represent the placement of each village on the survey responses for Conflict and for Cooperation. Column 3 provides our interpretation of the anthropological studies of social processes in villages falling within each pair of boxes.

As an indication of the changes taking place within a 5-year period, we found that 5 of our 12 villages had shifted from one block to another from 1964 to 1969.

If we had relied on either surveys or anthropological methods alone, it would have been impossible to carry out this analysis. If I had had only the student's anthropological report on Mito and had noticed his characterization of the village as low in both conflict and cooperation, I would not have known what to make of that finding.

If I only had the survey to go by, I might not have noticed the apparent anomaly. If I had noticed it and then gone on to correlate the conflict and cooperation scores, the zero correlation might have made me assume that there were technical problems with the questionnaire or with the field survey interviewing.

TABLE 9.1 CONFLICT-COOPERATION TYPOLOGY

1	2	3
CONFLICT	*COOPERATION*	*SOCIAL PROCESSES*
Low	High	Integrated village moving ahead with broad sharing of costs and benefits
High	High	Factional strife but projects moving ahead with unequal sharing of costs and benefits
High	Low	Divisions too sharp to permit much progress but factional leaders still struggling
Low	Low	Village going nowhere. Potential leaders have given up struggle

Here we had encountered a real theoretical breakthrough—an unusual case in which a zero correlation was statistically significant because it proved that the accepted thinking of the relations between conflict and cooperation was simply wrong. Even then, it would have been hard for me to imagine the social characteristics of each village that fell in a particular box. It was only after we went back to reread the anthropological reports that we were able to conclude that the fit between the survey scores and the anthropological studies of social processes "made sense."

Our system also enabled us to explain some of the changes from cooperation to conflict in the 5-year period. For example, in the case of Huayopampa shifting to high conflict and high cooperation, we found that the men and women of the younger generation had achieved such high education levels that they had left for professional education in Lima. Without the young people to help them in farming, the parents were struggling to combine their farming tasks with their service to community cooperative enterprises. That strain was coming to frustrate them more and more.

The lesson of this case indicates that sociologists should not give up on surveys. We only need to recognize its limitations in studies of organizations and communities. As others have pointed out, if we combine surveys with social anthropological studies, we will find that the surveys enrich the anthropological studies and the anthropological data enrich the survey data by showing how attitudes, values, and perceptions measured are reflected in behavior.

In the past, sociologists who concentrated on survey methods recognized the value of some preliminary interviewing in order to help them to formulate relevant questions, but then they left fieldwork aside and simply concentrated on the presentation and analysis of survey data. Our experience indicates that flexibly structured interviewing should not only precede the surveys but should also follow up to help us to explain what the surveys suggest. The process should not be one-two but rather going back and forth between the two types of data to get the most out of this combination.

We should not think of surveys and case studies in terms of quantification versus qualitative studies. In two of the villages studied, our fieldworkers gathered solid data on family income, on the amount of land owned, on the farm tools and equipment owned, on whether only family members worked on the farm or whether there was hired help part-time. Other village studies provided some but not all of these data.

The purposes of your research should determine the methods used. If your purpose is to predict how people will vote in a presidential election, a good survey is enough. If you want to discover why they will vote in the way predicted, a more extensive case study can provide important additional information.

If you want to discover how various variables are related to each other, a statistical correlational analysis will give you that answer. On the other hand, if you want to learn how you or others should intervene in that situation to produced a desired change, you will have to go beyond surveys into intensive case studies. Can a case study produce generalizable findings? We will consider that question in Chapter 12.

CHAPTER TEN

ON HISTORY: HOW THE PAST SHAPES PRESENT AND FUTURE

Our Peruvian village studies opened my eyes to the value of history in social research. Up to this point, I had seen history as just incidental background for understanding present day communities or organizations. Now I came to see history as providing essential data on the formation of today's communities.

I thought I was catering only to the interests of Peruvian students by suggesting that they limit their interest to events within the last 50 years. The students refused to accept the 50 year limit and in some cases probed up to 500 years in the history of villages or areas.

The Paradox Of The Mantaro Valley

The understanding of the participative paradox of the Mantaro Valley required us to go back to the conquest of Peru. In the Chancay Valley, we traced the beginnings of the differentiation of Huayopampa from Pacaraos back more than a century.

In the culture and social structure of the highlands of Peru, the Mantaro Valley departs sharply from the general pattern of mestizos, owning large haciendas, controlling political power, and dominating the indigenous population. In the 1960s, the Mantaro Valley was populated by small farmers, merchants, and small businessmen, and the villages were characterized by a high degree of grassroots participatory democracy.

When Pizarro and his small band of conquerors reached the Mantaro Valley in 1532, they were surprised and alarmed to be faced by several thousand Huancas. The natives were not there to do battle but rather to seek an alliance with the Spaniards. The Huancas had been independent up to 1460, when the Incas conquered them and incorporated them into the Inca empire. In Pizarro's time, the Huancas still regarded the Incas as their enemies.

After five days of feasting, drinking, and dancing, the Spaniards and the Huancas signed a treaty whereby, in return for Spanish military support, the Huancas were guaranteed continued possession of their lands and local autonomy.

After Pizarro's death, the treaty was disregarded as Spaniards moved in to take over large stretches of land. Huanca delegates complained in vain to governmental authorities in Lima. In 1560, two Huanca leaders made their way to Spain with the treaty and secured an audience with King Philip II. The king upheld the treaty with a decree that the haciendas already established be eliminated and that, in the future, no Spaniards should be allowed to own large estates in that area (Espinosa, 1973).

Late in the nineteenth century, the opening up of large mining operations in the mountains just to the west of the Valley drew the sons of Mantaro Valley farmers into industrial work and also into unionization. As the sons moved back and forth between the mines and the family homes, the young miners brought back the spirit of protest and indigenous development to the villages.

In 1908, the Central Railroad from Lima to Huancayo was completed, and in the early 1930s the central highway from Lima to Huancayo was built. These major transportation links stimulated the movement of merchandise, people, and ideas through the central highlands and to the coast, where Peru's industrial development was concentrated.

Origins Of The Differentiation Between Huayopampa And Pacaraos

In the Chancay Valley, we contrasted two communities, Pacaraos (at an altitude of 10,000 feet above sea level) and Huayopampa (at 6,000 feet). In the early years of the twentieth century, both villages were populated by subsistence farmers, cultivating the traditional crops of corn and potatoes. In the 1940s, villagers from Huayopampa built a road down to the thickly settled coastal delta, which made it possible to switch their farming into tropical fruits and get them to coastal markets. (Pacaraos was too cold to support tropical fruits.)

Altitude was not the only differentiating factor. Huayopampa stood out among all the villages in the highlands of the Chancay Valley in its educational development and in cooperative community organization.

A Catholic missionary school was established in Huayopampa in 1850. Although it was short-lived, it raised the literacy level above that of other villages in the area. When petitions to the government brought no action, in 1886 Huayopampa built its own school and hired a teacher. It was 1922 before any other village in this area had its own school.

In 1904, Huayopampa built a new school and attracted as teachers a remarkable couple, the Ceferino Villars. Since their two sons succeeded them, Huayopampa remained under the influence of the Villars family until 1925.

The pattern of education established by the Villars family differed markedly from the traditional Peruvian pattern of rote learning and the glorification of national leaders. The children studied the flora and fauna, archaeology, and history of the area. Teachers led the pupils to understand and appreciate the local community and its culture. In contrast to the individualistic orientation of education elsewhere, the Villars stressed the collective arrangements of their indigenous past. They organized the children into work groups, with elected leaders, for maintenance work in and around the school. They emphasized the value and dignity of manual labor, establishing school garden plots and a reforestation project where pupils integrated what they had learned from their farm families with information and ideas the teachers introduced from agricultural research and extension. The teachers linked up Huayopampa with the National Agrarian University on the coast to provide information and guidance for the development of tropical fruit culture.

In Pacaraos, only two of the ten teachers were natives of the village, and only one played an active role in village affairs. In Huayopampa, all the teachers were natives of the village, and all were quite active in village affairs.

Pacaraos was dominated by one family that owned a trucking enterprise and a small business. In Huayopampa, wealth and power were much more broadly distributed. The village water and electric power system were cooperatively built and owned, as were the village store and trucking business. Largely due to the profits in tropical fruit, the average family income in Huayopampa was on a level with white-collar worker income in Lima.

On The Uses Of History

When we studied these villages in the 1960s, it would have been impossible to understand them outside of the context of their histories.

The democratic dynamism of the Mantaro Valley villages was built on the structural changes that were imposed by the Spanish crown in the sixteenth century in eliminating large haciendas in that region. The spirit of collective solidarity and indigenous protest was stimulated by the labor union experience of the children of the Mantaro Valley farmers.

In the Chancay Valley, the early and continuing dedication to education was built out of the Catholic missionary school in 1850 and then nourished and strengthened by the family of the Ceferino Villars from 1904 to 1925. Furthermore, the cooperative culture of Huayopampa was built upon the leadership of the Villars, emphasizing cooperative organization and dedication to the values of the early indigenous culture.

Other villages in the Huayopampa area had also developed successful tropical fruit cultivation. At least one other, the village of Lampian, had a highly influential school teacher in the early years of the twentieth century, but he emphasized the values of individualism over collective solidarity. The young men of Lampian left the community to earn their living in coastal cities.

Let me add this note on historiography: For the early history of the Mantaro Valley, we relied on a professional Peruvian historian, Waldemar Espinosa. The village histories were provided us by students of social anthropology. In the mid-nineteenth century, few villagers were literate, but there was usually one who could read and write and thus keep records, which students found in village archives. (For a full account of our village studies, see Whyte and Alberti, 1976.)

When we carried out our studies of the Mondragón cooperatives in the Basque country of Spain from 1975 to 1991, our approach was influenced by our commitment to history in the 1960s. Instead of simply concentrating on the current scene and recent developments, we focused major attention on the history of Mondragón and the cooperatives.

Our venture into history taught us certain lessons for future historical studies; for example, not to become so fixated on the big national picture that local and regional studies is neglected. Remember that past events—sometimes remote past events—can be essential to explain what is now observed.

In a literate society, the social researcher will find readily available media and documentary records, but even if only a person or two is literate in a village we study, that local record can provide essential information on past events that are shaping what we observe in field studies.

We should recognize that even a single individual can have an enormous effect on the future development of his village. That was the case of Ceferino Villars (supported by his family) in Huayopampa.

Also, we should recognize that the nature of educational development in a village can play a major role in the social and economic development of the village. That was not only the case of Huayopampa but also in the neighboring community of Lampian. Whereas the social and economic development of Huayopampa was shaped by the Villars in a cooperative framework, in Lampian the principal teacher also had a major role in orienting the pupils in an individualistic direction. The result was that Lampian students left the village early to seek jobs in the delta and in Lima, the Huayopampa students stayed with their village until they could leave for professional education on the coast.

CHAPTER ELEVEN
LEARNING FROM MONDRAGÓN

Our studies of the Mondragón cooperative complex built on several themes. In the first place, we focused primary attention on the *history* of the development of the complex. We noted the special importance of a single individual in guiding and shaping the complex. We showed how particular *social inventions* brought about change and growth within the complex. We developed the project within a framework for the study of organizational cultures.

I first encountered Mondragón on the bulletin board outside of economics professor Jaroslav Vanek's office. There was a clipping by Robert Oakshott on "Mondragón: Spain's Oasis of Democracy," from the London *Observer*, January 21, 1973. I had never heard of anything like this: a dynamic complex of worker cooperatives that was continuing to grow. I resolved that I would have to go there to see for myself. Ana Gutierrez Johnson, a graduate student from Peru, went with Kathleen and me for our first two weeks in Mondragón in 1975. Ana stayed on for 7 weeks more, gathering material for a master's thesis, and in later study trips she completed work on a doctoral thesis. I had assumed that Ana and I would collaborate on a book on Mondragón; I had written six draft chapters that I sent to Ana, then in Costa Rica. When she returned to Cornell, she told me that she wanted to write her own book.

That was a blow, but it turned out to be a lucky break for me. If I now wanted to continue with my own book, I would have to plunge in further with my own fieldwork. Also, since Ana's last trip, the cooperatives had encountered some setbacks, and it seemed important to find out how they were adjusting to adversity.

Kathleen had edited my first book, had closely followed my industrial studies and had been with me on much of my fieldwork in Latin America and had participated in my interviews in Mondragón. I suggested that we work together on the Mondragón book.

The study of the Mondragón cooperatives was the last field study I was able to undertake, as advancing age and postpolio syndrome was draining the energy from my legs. It absorbed my interest over a number of years, from 1975 to 1991 (Whyte & Whyte 1988, 1991). That project produced perhaps my best book, after *Street Corner Society*.

This experience enriched my knowledge of research methods and social theory. I extended my understanding of history through studying the origins of the cooperatives from the end of the Spanish Civil War in 1939, and on into the development of the first worker cooperative in 1956, and then through the various stages of development of the cooperative complex of worker and consumer cooperatives, including a bank, a research and development institute, an organization to cover social security and insurance, and an educational system. From its beginning in 1956, the cooperative complex had grown to over 26,000 members in 1994.

The historical focus enabled us to work out a systematic study of the *culture* of the cooperatives, at a time when students of organizational behavior and practitioners were giving increased attention to the examination of organizational cultures. Through field interviewing and documents, we put the various pieces together. We also saw them emerging and developing through time.

It was the Mondragón project that led me to focus on *social inventions* as a neglected and important factor in guiding social change. In my presidential address to the American Sociological Association in 1981 on "Social Inventions for Solving Human Problems," I defined a social invention as

- a new element in organizational structure or interorganizational relations;
- new sets of procedures for shaping human interactions and activities and the relations of humans to the natural and social environment;
- a new policy in action (that is, not just on paper); or
- a new role or set of roles.

When I announced the topic, one sociologist congratulated me on focusing on *social interventions*. I responded that it was not my intention to focus on interventions, which are brought onto people by outsiders. I wanted to learn from studying the *social inventions* that people developed in diagnosing the problems they were facing.

Mondragón provided a wealth of examples of *social inventions*. In fact, many of them were the creation of the founder, Father José María Arizmendiarrieta. Through focusing on the most remarkable man I have ever known, I learned about how he was able to shape and guide the development of the Mondragón cooperative complex.

He also provided us with essential clues for understanding the *social processes* that guided the growth and development of the cooperatives. With that initial information, one would think that Don José María was an eloquent and charismatic leader. That was not the case. His early followers reported that his sermons were dull and hard to follow. His greatest strengths were in stimulating dialogue and developing the abilities of those who conversed with him to analyze their social and economic problems.

The process began when he first organized a group of working-class youths and their parents to establish a vocational school in industrial arts. (Beginning with a 2-year course, the Escuela Politecnica Profesional eventually built a program of college and postcollege studies of engineering.)

Don José María was not content simply with building a new institution. He remained in constant touch with the young men who had worked with him in the beginning. One of his closest associates remembers that "in the calculations we were making in 1956 we counted more than 2,000 circles of study that he conducted. Some for religious and humanistic orientation; others for social orientation."

Thus, from 1941 on, Don José María conducted at least one study session every 2.7 days, not counting holidays and vacations. As one of his former students told us, "He taught classes in religion and sociology—and really his religion classes were mainly sociology" (Whyte & Whyte, pp.32–33). Some sessions focused on conflicts between labor and capital, reform of private enterprise, and self-management and the participation of workers in ownership.

In pursuing these seminars, Don José María was building a vital element of the organizational culture, the practice of full discussion of plans and past performance. He asked his followers to look ahead and plan for the future. Javier Retegui, who in 1975 was director of the Escuela Politecnica Professional, said to us about his mentor, "He sees the future and makes us face it." Don José María told us, "I have no power." If we mean power in terms of holding an executive position, that is technically correct. He never held any title other than "Advisor." On the other hand, he had enormous influence. He studied and reflected on the problems of social and economic development and then weighed in with his advice—which was often, but not always, followed.

Don José María embraced neither the ideologies of capitalism nor socialism. He dreamed of a peaceful social revolution through which all social classes could work together for common objectives.

He can best be described as a *pragmatist*. His orientation was strikingly similar to that of John Dewey in the conceptualization of practical options within a democratic and highly participative framework (see Westbrook, 1991).

That meant adjusting his hopes to what became organizationally possible. In our interviews and in the cooperatives documents, we often encountered the key concept of *equilibrio*, referring to the need to adjust social plans to economic forces, and to technical requirements.

The Social Councils of the various cooperatives have become major forums for the stimulation of discussion of what *equilibrio* means in practice. They were one of the first social inventions of Don José María. Like other cooperatives elsewhere, Mondragón has its Governing Council or Board of Directors elected by the members as well as an elected Auditing Council. Members are chosen for the Governing Council in at-large voting. Members of the Social Council are elected from work groups or departments, and they have come to be considered as representing the members as workers, whereas the Governing Council has come to be considered the principal representative of the workers as owners.

Why have two councils representing the same body of people? When people have to consider at the same time their long run interests as owners against their more immediate concerns about working conditions and systems of compensation and other matters affecting them as workers, this puts them in an ambivalent position. Ambivalence is a poor position from which to make decisions. The separation of owner from worker interests helps to insure that worker interests are thoroughly debated and studied in the Social Councils.

Although the Social Councils are only advisory bodies, in some cooperatives they have become highly influential in affecting policy decisions of the cooperatives. In some cases, where the Social Councils took a position against the Governing Council, the annual assembly of all members has supported the Social Council, overruling the decision of the Governing Council. In other cases, there has been discussion by leaders of the two councils that resulted in adjustments of the Governing Council to Social Council positions.

In some ways, the Social Councils have become like U.S. unions that cooperate with management on many points but oppose them on others. The Social Councils do not have the power to call the members out on strike, but they do have the power, lacking to U.S. unions, to appeal to all worker members to overrule Governing Councils decisions.

The first and perhaps the most important of José María's social inventions arose out of his early Seminary studies of the history of worker cooperatives. He was inspired by the vision of Robert Owen and the other English pioneers who adopted the Rochdale Principles, but then he noted that, although consumer cooperatives had survived and grown, the Owen worker cooperative textile mill had eventually been taken over by private investors. Why had this happened? Ownership of that cooperative was based upon stock, one share for each original worker. With the passing of time, as some members left and wanted to sell their stock, and as the company needed money to expand, private investors bought up the stock and gained control.

How could that be avoided? The answer was to eliminate stock. The initial capital of a worker cooperative would be based on *loans* to the enterprise by each worker (the loans being paid off in deductions from worker pay). These *loans* were then used to set up *capital accounts* in the name of each worker. After a percentage of profits was set aside as a reserve fund, the remainder was transferred to the *capital account* of each worker. Control was not to be determined by stock but simply by being a full time worker in the cooperative. (In profitable times, the profits were shared with the members, being added to their *capital accounts*.)

This meant that no Mondragón cooperative could be taken over by stockholders because there was no stock. This was a striking invention. In the United States, the plywood cooperatives of the Northwest were long considered highly successful, but few of them exist today. They have either gone bankrupt or have been taken over by private investors, who bought the stock of retiring workers or of those who quit their jobs.

These *capital accounts* also serve to provide the cooperatives with flexibility in financing. When the cooperative is losing money, the members do not need to shut down or sell out to private capital. Their first recourse can be voting to sacrifice some percentage of their capital accounts so as to replenish the firm's reserve funds. The members generally will prefer to keep their jobs rather than save on their capital accounts.

Don José María recognized the need of the cooperatives for new investment money without surrendering control to private firms or banks. Shortly after Ulgor, the first worker cooperative, was established, he began persuading their leaders that they would need to have their own cooperative bank. They rejected the idea; when they were just learning how to be good managers of a manufacturing firm, they had no time or interest in such a project. Don José María persisted. When he was unable to persuade them, for the first and only time in his experience with the cooperatives, he imposed his decision on them. Spanish law for the creation of a bank calls first for a preorganization meeting, a statement of the purposes of the bank, and the signature of two of the founders. For the preorganization meeting, which was never held, Don José María signed the names of two of the leaders of Ulgor.

We asked the man who told us this story, were not those men upset with Don José María? He said that they were a bit annoyed at the start, but they thought it would never amount to anything. The Caja Laboral Popular became the first engine of growth of the cooperatives and grew to be the largest and most prosperous saving bank in the Basque country.

A savings bank or credit union was and is a familiar institution, but, with the Caja, the social invention involved a new purpose for the organization. Most credit unions specialize in loans to individual consumers. The Caja does do individual consumer loans, but its primary purposes are the financing of new cooperatives and the emergency assistance to cooperatives in financial difficulties. For these purposes, the Caja set up its Entrepreneurial Division, which helps new groups to establish their cooperatives and also serves to work with failing cooperatives through its Intervention Department. Up through 1994, only a tiny percentage of the Mondragón firms have failed and gone out of business. Around 1990, two small cooperatives, in severe financial difficulties, voted to sell their firms to private investors. All of the largest cooperatives and cooperative groups have survived.

Don José María and his followers believed that maintaining organizational democracy depended on keeping organizations small. Their ideal seemed to be a firm with not more than 500 members. In fact, in its early years, Ulgor was so successful in the Spanish market that it had grown to over 3,000 members by 1974. Significantly, the only strike in Mondragón firms was centered in Ulgor. It only lasted a few days and only involved about 400 members, but nevertheless it spurred Mondragón's leaders to think of new ways to grow and yet remain close to worker members.

In the 1960s, the cooperatives took the first step in this direction. By this time, several new cooperatives had been formed from firms producing components for Ulgor. Here Don José María provided the social invention of *cooperative groups.* So that each new firm would not have to build its own personnel department, accounting department, and legal services, the first cooperative group called ULARCO was formed from the firms initially arising out of Ulgor. Under its new name of FAGOR, this cooperative group is the oldest and most successful of all the cooperative groups. It is also the one most closely integrated, with all individual firms sharing in the distribution of profits and losses.

To stimulate the development of new cooperative groups, the Caja offered to pay half of the extra cost of the new group management for three years. Within a short time, nearly all of the cooperatives had joined together in their own cooperative group.

To keep the cooperatives up to date with new technological developments, Don José María encouraged school teacher Manuel Quevedo and his associates in the Escuela Politecnica Profesional to go out to the cooperatives to study their existing technologies and possible future technical innovations. Following this, he persuaded the Governing Council of the Escuela to support this group for visits to industrial research and development centers in France.

In 1974, Don José María proposed that the cooperatives establish their own R&D center for technological development. As one of the leaders of Ulgor put it, "We opposed this idea when Don José María first presented it to us, but he always succeeded in convincing us." With support from the Caja and other cooperatives, Ikerlan, the industrial technical research program was established. Ikerlan moved into its new $2 million building in

1977. It has since expanded, with financial support from the regional Basque government and from contract research with private firms. Ikerlan is now so highly regarded that it has come to be involved in international science and engineering research programs in Europe.

Don José María did not invent consumer cooperatives, but he did invent a new structure for worker-consumer cooperatives. Members of the Governing Council of Eroski are elected on a 50-50 basis from Eroski workers and consumers. By its statutes, the chairman of the Governing Council must always be a consumer member.

Don José María also took the initiative to establish the structure of worker-farmer cooperatives, with their Governing Councils chosen on an equal basis by producing farmers and by those packaging and selling the farm produce.

Don José María died in 1976, but the organizational culture his initiatives had created carried on without him. The leaders of the cooperatives created new structures to adapt to expected changes in conditions.

Up until 1987, the Caja had been the only organization holding all the cooperatives together, as each of them signed agreements to do their banking with the Caja and to organize themselves in the standard form established by the first cooperatives. To bind the firms together more effectively socially and economically, in 1987 the Cooperative Congress of Mondragón Cooperatives was formed, with representatives of each firm, and with an elected governing council to act between the biennial Congress meetings.

At the same time, the leaders began the process of linking the firms more closely together in terms of sharing common markets or common technologies. In 1991, the Mondragón Cooperative Corporation was set up, with an elected president and vice president of each of the nine divisions.

From the mid-1970s into the mid-1980s, Mondragón cooperatives especially in manufacturing went through difficult periods, with some of them kept alive through intervention of the Caja, and overall manufacturing employment went down—in line with worldwide trends.

By 1990, largely through rapid expansion of the Caja, Eroski, and other service organizations, the downward trend in employment had been reversed. In 1996 total employment was at a record level of over 28,000, and there has been a new surge of growth of manufacturing firms.

When I first reported on Mondragón at the 1976 annual meeting of the American Sociological Association, a discussant denied that the case had any general relevance. He said that Mondragón's success had been due to Basque culture and to a particular leader; since that culture and that individual could not be created elsewhere, the Mondragón case was just a colorful story.

I pondered that question. How much did the Basque culture explain? Indeed the Basques do seem more inclined than other cultures to create worker cooperatives. In the 1980s, there were more Basque cooperatives outside of the Mondragón system than within it. In line with the Basque tradition of forming small working groups, all of these cooperatives outside of the Mondragón system were small and independent of each other. Only Mondragón had an integrated and mutually reenforcing system—and there was no precedent in the Basque country or elsewhere for such a system.

Furthermore, the Mondragón model has been copied in Valencia, in southern Spain, with quite a different culture from the Basques (A. Martinez, 1991). *El Grup Cooperatiu de Valencia* was founded in the early 1970s, after the Valencia people had been to Mondragón and studied its cooperatives. The Valencia group has its own savings bank and educational system, and links together manufacturing and service firms. The Valencia complex has been expanding rapidly into the 1990s.

Students of worker cooperatives are agreed that an isolated cooperative firm, surrounded by a universe of private enterprises, has poor prospects for success and survival. No other cooperative complex has developed the extensive system of mutually supporting organizations, but elsewhere cooperative groups have been seeking to establish links with independent organizations that might serve them.

Students of cooperatives have been making pilgrimages to Mondragón, and we find some features of Mondragón being applied elsewhere. David Ellerman of the Industrial Cooperative Association of Boston developed legislation for applying the Mondragón social invention of *capital accounts* in Massachusetts, and that legislation has been enacted in New York and several other states.

Although Don José María and his work cannot be duplicated elsewhere, we can focus on the nature of his contributions. He provided a *vision* of the kinds of organizations they were all seeking to build, he established a *social process* to enable his associates to critique what they had done, and to plan future changes. He also established the *equilibrio* principal for guiding future development of social and technical and economic development.

When Don José María completed his seminary studies, he petitioned his Bishop to send him to the University of Louvain in Belgium for postgraduate work in sociology. Fortunately, the Bishop turned him down and sent him to the small town of Mondragón, where he became one of the most extraordinary *applied sociologists* of all time and all places.

———————————————•◦•———————————————

Organizational culture appears to be a very ephemeral topic. How can we get down to cases to make the culture of any given organization quite concrete—and revealed in behavior and in documents?

From 1975 onward, I have been speculating about the nature of the culture of the Mondragón cooperatives. As we were writing our book, I wrote out a first draft of my cultural interpretation. I showed it to Davydd Greenwood, who, during the months of July in 1985 and 1986, was conducting a seminar on research methods and social theories for 15 members of the personnel and human resources departments of FAGOR. He found it interesting and shared it with several of the FAGOR people who could read English. They had criticisms but thought that it would be useful for the seminar to have it translated into Spanish.

By this time, the Greenwood 1985 seminar had evolved into a *participatory action research* (PAR) project, focusing on a study of the social and cultural history of Ulgor, Mondragón's oldest and largest cooperative. As the seminar studied what various outsiders had written about Mondragón, my essay received major attention. Their critiques helped me to rewrite and strengthen my cultural analysis. Thus, we can say that the cultural interpretation presented in our books is to some extent an integration of the views of outside students and of the interpretation of those within the system—although we did not agree on all points.

We described the culture in Whyte and Whyte (1989, 1991). To us, the key elements are the *cognitive framework* and the *shaping systems*.

The *cognitive framework* is the set of ideas and beliefs about basic values, organizational objectives, and guiding principles that form the foundation of any organization. *Shaping systems* enable an organizational culture to be maintained or changed. These are major policies, structures, and instruments of governance and management.

We learned about the culture through interviews and documents and checking our interpretations with people in the complex. As we look back on that description in our books, it has occurred to us that we should now include *social processes* as among the elements of *shaping systems*.It was the social processes initiated by Don José María that shaped the course of development of the complex—the openness of communications and the frequent discussions to review past progress and plan for the future that kept the complex true to its basic values.

Our organizational cultural analysis primarily is based on interviews with Don José María and the leaders of the early stages of development of the complex. For a study of the history of the complex, that focus was necessary for we were concentrating on people who were intimately involved in establishing the social, cultural, and technological bases of the complex.

That approach necessarily involves a bias toward seeing the complex as its principal early leaders saw it. To some extent, we can guard against that bias by citing the experience of Davydd Greenwood with the PAR projects focusing on the development of Ulgor and FAGOR. Beyond the interview seminar members conducted with a range of members, the seminar brought together discussion groups representing a wide variety of experience—early members and those recently hired, high and low ranking members, white-collar and blue-collar workers.

We particularly were impressed with what we learned from those recently hired members. Some said that, when they got hired, they were just looking for a job and knew little or nothing about the cooperatives. Now, however, they had fully grasped the values and guiding principles of the system. They endorsed the organizational culture laid out for them, but they complained that, in some instances, the supervisors and personnel people were not living up to those values and guiding principles.

Any study of organizational culture must include some treatment of the role of individual leadership. In our books and in this chapter, we have focused our attention on the role of the principal leader. We have seen how he provided a *vision*, a series of *social inventions*, and the development of *social processes* that still guide the Mondragón cooperatives.

Have we made a useful and reasonably valid interpretation of the culture of the cooperatives, based particularly on our studies of the FAGOR cooperative group? That remains to be seen in future judgments of outside critics and of members of the cooperatives.

Can the methods we used to arrive at this description of the culture of the Mondragón cooperatives be used for the study of other organizations—particularly private companies and corporations? If others are interested in trying out such a methodology, we hope that it may be useful and even lead them to improving on our framework.

CHAPTER TWELVE

SOCIOLOGY AS SOCIAL SCIENCE

When I began my first field study in the North End of Boston, during my Junior Fellowship period at Harvard (1936–40), I assumed that sociology was—or should become—a science. In that setting at that time, physics was thought to provide the model of a true science. *The Logic of Modern Physics* (Bridgman, 1927) seemed to be the last word on defining the nature of science. According to Bridgman, the operations must be subject to measurement. Quantification was the basic requirement of science.

It was not only sociologists who felt inferior to physicists. In an earlier period, many biologists felt this same sense of inferiority and therefore a need to ape the physicists (Mayr, 1983). The extraordinary advances of biology in recent decades have eliminated any question regarding the scientific legitimacy of work in that field, but it seems to me that many sociologists are still trying to follow the physics model—as its logic was laid down by Bridgman in the 1920s.

The history of biology may help to liberate sociologists from the physics model. I am not suggesting that sociologists should follow the biological model—or that of any other science—but biology does indicate that scientific research can involve *qualitative* as well as *quantitative* studies.

As Ernest Mayr, the eminent biologist and historian of science points out, some of biological research involves experimentation and yields quantitative results, but evolutionary biology is not subject to quantification. Similarly, when the biologist is dealing with relational phenomena, such as species, classification, ecosystems, communicatory behavior, and regulation, these judgments are basically *qualitative*.

According to Mayr, advances in biological sciences have depended in large measure upon improvements in systems of classification. These advances have depended upon shifting from conventional or common sense classifications to systems more useful to scientific research.

Here we should consider the difference between *explanation* and *interpretation*. As I see it, explanation refers to processes and results that can reasonably be observed and documented. Interpretation involves a theoretical statement regarding why certain events happened or certain results were achieved. Interpretation is a *cumulative* activity; it draws tentative conclusions from one case that might apply to other cases. Insofar as these interpretations fit other cases, they gain validity. The best interpretation is not a firm scientific conclusion, but, when applied to human relations, such interpretations are the best tools for further guidance for actions.

The same trend as in biology can be shown in the advances of organizational behavior research. The early exponents of the doctrine of scientific management claimed that the same general principles governed all types of organizations.

In a study of 203 manufacturing firms, British sociologist Joan Woodward (1965) first tried to determine the factors influencing the structure of industrial organizations and patterns of line-staff relations. She found enormous variability among firms and no clear patterns. She only struck pay dirt when she focused on types of technology, which she classified as unit or small batch, mass production, and continuous process operations. Now she found systematic relations between certain types of technology and certain aspects of formal organization and staff-line relations. This is an impressive example of the need to advance in systems of classification before being able to make useful quantitative operations. Here, the *qualitative* operation necessarily precedes *quantitative* research. This raises a number of questions which I shall seek to answer in the following pages.

How do we structure our qualitative research? If we want to quantify (as I do), what do we quantify? How do we quantify certain aspects of behavior or the attitudes and perceptions of the people we are studying? If we seek to measure attitudes through surveys, can we link those measures to observed behavior?

Does the researcher work alone or as part of a group? In the latter case, how can the group be organized to maximize the mutual learning? What is the role of the leader of such a group?

What is the relationship between basic research and applied research? Can a given project yield basic research findings while at the same time advancing practical objectives?

To answer that question, I quote from Chester I. Barnard's comments on the National Science Foundation's attempt to distinguish between the two types of research (*Scientific American*, Nov. 1957):

> ...[As one] example, we have Karl Jansky's discovery of radio signals from outer space. Jansky, according to the report was not engaged in basic research; he merely made a basic discovery. Here the confusion arises from labeling research according to the motives for which it is carried on; there is an element of snobbery involved which should not be encouraged. After all Louis Pasteur made his great contributions to the foundations of bacteriology in trying to find solutions for the practical problems of the French silk and wine industries....
>
> ...The full story would require display of the interdependence between basic and applied research and would not minimize the fact that traffic in inspiration, ideas and technique moves in both directions.

A good case study can advance sociological knowledge. With that claim, I argue against the conventional wisdom that holds that each case is unique so that no general conclusions can be drawn from it. While a case may provide interesting insights, that is not the same as scientific proof; scientific advances rest upon statistical correlations, according to that line of argument.

While each case, as a whole, is unique, a good case offers certain parts that can be duplicated elsewhere in quite different circumstances. That was the case with my study of the informal structure of street corner gangs. I assume that we can apply that analysis to any informal group whose members interact together for an extended period of time; a pattern of leadership emerges in which one individual initiates changes in group activity or assents to the proposals of others—if he does not assent, no change in activity takes place. I would expect this to happen in every instance except when a leadership change is about to take place—in other words, I would expect this pattern to be maintained up to 90 percent of the time of observation. Whether I am right or wrong can be checked by others, who make the same observations I made—which is the essence of the scientific process.

In that case study of Mondragón, we can derive an important *uniformity*: if you organize your worker cooperative on the customary basis of having each original member buy a share of stock, that cooperative will eventually degenerate into a private enterprise even if it is financially successful for some time. Mondragón provided the world with an alternative financial structure, basing control on the members, without any stock being issued. As we have seen, this model has been adopted in legislation in several states.

During my graduate student days (1940–42) at the University of Chicago, I encountered a variation of the case study issue. At that time, the most popular debate among sociological faculty members was between those promoting statistics versus those supporting case studies. Within that department, the principal proponent of statistics was Samuel Stouffer and his case study opponent was Herbert Blumer. That argument was extended nationally in a meeting of the American Sociological Association, where Blumer squared off with George Lundberg. That was such a sharp argument that, when the two shook hands at the end, it conveyed the misleading impression that there were no hard feelings.

Those debates were gripping drama, but they left me unsatisfied regarding my own case study of *Street Corner Society*. I was not prepared to settle for *understanding*. I liked Stouffer better than Blumer, and I saw the merits of quantitative measures—but measures of what? At the time, sociologists and social psychologists were concentrating on the measurement of subjective phenomena: attitudes, perceptions, and values. On the street corners of Boston's North End, I wanted to focus directly on behavior rather than on how people felt and thought about that behavior.

Long after my North End study, I came to see the value of surveys, especially when used in connection with intensive interviewing and observation methods, as I described the process in our Peruvian village studies.

For studies of social processes that develop and change through time, surveys are of very limited use. You can make comparisons of survey figures from one date to another, as we did in those village studies, but you need the interviewing and observational data coming out of *qualitative* studies.

Compared to my street corner studies, the study of large scale industrial organizational changes taking place through months or years presents a much more complex research problem. Can we make this adaptation?

Let me illustrate, with a case study several of us at Cornell have been making of the transformation of the Xerox Corporation. Based on the invention of Xerography, Xerox grew and prospered spectacularly from the 1960s through the 1970s. As patent protection ran out, competitors in Japan and the U.S. began steadily to reduce the Xerox market share in photocopiers. By the early 1980s, there seemed a real chance that the company that invented the process might just be reduced to distributing copiers produced elsewhere.

Beginning in the late 1970s, Xerox carried out a far reaching transformation of its organizational culture, including major structural and social process changes. By the mid-1980s, Xerox had ended is shrinkage in market share and had begun to gain back some of its previous losses. In 1989, among major companies, Xerox had won the Baldrige National Award for high quality organizational performance.

Some of us documented the early stages of this transformation, focusing on union-management cooperation to reduce manufacturing costs (Klingel & Martin, 1989; Whyte, Greenwood, & Lazes, 1989; Whyte, 1989). At this time, we broadened the scope of our studies to encompass the transformation process from top management down to workers and going beyond manufacturing to examine changes in the engineering and the distribution and service organizations. Under the leadership of Frank Wayno, whose first report was titled *The Road to the Baldrige Award: Human Resources Aspects of the Transformation of the Xerox Corporation*, we were in effect following the course of changes over more than a decade, throughout the various departments of the company and in its union-management relations.

We were seeking answers to two questions, (a) how had the transformation of Xerox been brought about? and (b) to what extent could conclusions drawn from this single case study be utilized to provide practical advice to other major companies facing the types of problems Xerox had faced?

By the time Frank Wayno began his study, the transformation had been carried through successfully, so all those who had played major roles in bringing about these changes were proud of what they and their associates had done and were happy to talk at length about the processes of change. With the permission of his informants, Wayno used a tape recorder for the interviews. With outside grant support, he was able to get secretarial services to transcribe the interviews. He gave that record back to each informant, to ask them if there was anything they wanted to change or add. This suggested to the informants that there were other key people who should be interviewed. Wayno followed up with further interviews, including three with men who had left the company for jobs or had retired.

When Wayno finished the first draft of the report, he gave copies to all his principal informants, asking them to read it, make notes on it, and then discuss it with him. This led to some major changes and even to some new people that he had to interview. We had been told that some of these busy executives would not want to read more than a one- or two-page memorandum, but every one of these people read it all and were eager to discuss it further with Wayno or others.

How do we arrive at tentative generalizations that might apply to other cases? A standard approach would be to state hypotheses and then test them statistically. In a complex case, evolving over more than a decade throughout the divisions of a large company, it would be impossible to state a hypothesis or set of hypotheses that would advance us toward the answers to our basic questions.

Our first step would be to depart from the theoretical studies of bureaucracies of mainstream sociologists. As I have noted Chapter 7, those not concerned with practical applications have been trying to devise theories that would apply to all types of bureaucracies, large and small, corporations and not for profit organizations. In effect, they were assuming a system of classification in which all those various organizations fit into a single category that they call a bureaucracy.

That makes as much sense as asking a plant scientist about the basic characteristics of vegetables. If he did not dismiss that as a foolish question, he might then go on to ask, "What vegetable are you interested in?" If we answer "potato," then he will want us to specify our interest further—nutritional properties, soil and climate conditions where potatoes are grown, yields per hectare in various countries, etc. Only as we get down to these classificatory questions can we advance our knowledge. The first step therefore is to limit the scope of our comparisons to similar phenomena, so that we will know what we are comparing with what.

Before they engage in systematic studies of any phenomena, biologists recognize the need to make *qualitative* judgments, placing the objects of study in a context of other similar phenomena. Only then do we begin to know what we are comparing with what.

For potential lessons to be drawn from the Xerox case, we wanted to limit the scope of the organizations considered to *large manufacturing firms heavily engaged in international trade*. A small manufacturing firm would not face the complexity of problems Xerox faced, and a firm in the service industries would be facing different problems from one in manufacturing. The emphasis on international trade is an important *qualitative* distinction, since firms competing only in local or regional areas might well survive with a variety of organizational patterns.

In the 1990s, through field research and the testimony of practitioners, we can recognize the central features of what I call "the new manufacturing organization." I contrast it with the mass production model that followed scientific management.

From the old to the new organization, I see the following changes taking place (Whyte, 1990, 1991).

From a Vertical (Command/Control) to a Horizontal (Workflow/ Sequential) Orientation. Instead of emphasizing the output of each department, managers and supervisors concentrated on developing and maintaining a smooth workflow of parts and operations from one unit to the next in line in the sequence. Instead of maintaining large stockpiles so that each department could operate independently, many of these large companies switched toward a just-in-time (JIT) policy. This meant ordering materials and components from vendors, at frequent intervals, so that the vendor supplies arrived shortly before they were needed.

The most obvious impact of JIT is to reduce drastically inventory costs, including the space required for temporary storage of stocks, and the additional movements to transport arriving materials into temporary storage and then getting them back when they were needed. Under the old model, deficiencies in operations could be overlooked, their sources buried under pressure to get on with production. Under the new model, the source of the problem becomes immediately apparent—not only to workers but also to staff engineers and supervisors, who converge to work with the operators to solve the problem. Furthermore, the need for finetuning the workflow leads management to train workers to observe indications of impending breakdowns. Problems located at their source and acted on immediately are much more likely to be solved than those that can be ignored while work goes on.

These changes have far reaching impacts on managerial policies and organizational structures. Under pressure of international competition, the emphasis shifts from maximum production to *high quality* and to meeting customer requirements for a greater variety of models.

To meet the new standards of quality and on-time delivery, manufacturers have been reducing sharply their numbers of suppliers. Instead of seeking to get suppliers competing with each other on price, companies are now beginning to work cooperatively with suppliers to help them achieve the high quality components needed.

Changing roles for supervisors and workers. Under the new model, focusing on sequential operations, it is impossible for supervisors to control closely their work operations. They must rely on workers to diagnose problems. This means shifting the emphasis from controlling workers to becoming a resource person, helping workers get the tools and supplies when they need them and consulting with them (and the engineers) when operational problems are beyond the immediate scope of worker skills.

As the emphasis shifts from individuals toward teamwork, supervisors have responsibilities to help workers to establish effective work teams. They also are expected to work with engineers as well as workers to help resolve problems that workers cannot solve on their own. These shifts in organizational structure and job responsibilities create a need to develop new and revised training programs for workers, supervisors and engineers. If the new manufacturing organization can be set up in a "greenfield" site, all of the interrelated parts can be planned together. If the new manufacturing organization is to be introduced into established plants and organizations, then companies face more complex problems of change—basically, how do they maintain operations for their current products while they put in place a new organizational system.

Discussion of the Xerox case could well take up a whole book, but for present purposes, let me concentrate on what seem to me the key features of this case.

Exposure of top officials to new organizational models. Here Xerox had the built-in advantage of joint ownership of a Japanese company, Fuji-Xerox. CEO David Kearns and other top U.S. Xerox officials visited Fuji-Xerox on several occasions and of course had full access to the Japanese partner's experience in its own highly successful transformation from a money losing operation to a highly profitable one, which had won the Deming award for high quality performance.

A personal and effective link between the corporate office and the production plants. When the Xerox top leadership decided on the general direction in which they wanted to go, they selected Harold Tragasch as their link from the production organization to middle management and corporate officers. Tragasch had a Ph.D. in psychology, specializing in social psychology, but his experience in Xerox was limited to the marketing organization and he had no experience in personnel. Through reading in the organizational behavior literature and discussions with organizational consultants and researchers, Tragasch was looking for ways to bring Xerox into line with this new strain of organizational thinking. At the plant operations level, Tragasch established close working relations with Dominic Argona in the personnel department, who was head of the *Organizational Effectiveness* unit in Manufacturing and with Anthony J. Costanza, the chief union leader for the Amalgamated Clothing and Textile Workers Union (ACTWU) in the Webster, New York, plants of Xerox.

Teamwork Days. How can *Employee Involvement* (EI) be extended from manufacturing into engineering, servicing and marketing units? Tragash and Larry Pace, assistant to Argona in Organizational Effectiveness in Manufacturing, devised a strategy beginning with *Teamwork Days*. For the first year, only manufacturing people participated, showing off exhibits of how they had worked out special problems within their unit. Tragash made certain that top officials of Xerox spent a day looking over the 40 exhibits and talking with those who had created them. This served to inform and stimulate top management people, and it also motivated heads of engineering, servicing, and marketing to mount their own programs. As *Teamwork Days* continued, Xerox had to transfer the events into a major convention hall to accommodate the exhibits and the crowds.

Diagnosing and resolving conflicts between preexisting management programs or conflicts with new elements being introduced. Tragasch and others working with him diagnosed some key problems and developed ways of dealing with them.

There was, for example, the need to adapt the system of evaluating the performance of managers from a focus exclusively upon the individual to one focused on teamwork. The aim was to find or develop *role model managers*. For this purpose, those building the new system had to locate within company operations an individual already regarded as a *role model manager* and study his behavior and how superiors and subordinates regarded him. For example, they found that the new *role model manager* should be a good teacher of subordinates and associates in order to help the organization to manage the increasing tempo of technical and organizational changes. Teaching ability had not been previously thought essential for a manager.

In the early 1980s, the company had found a vendor able to supply the wire-harnesses controlling the xerography process at a saving of $3.2 million per year. Management announced that six months later the wire-harness department would be shut down and about 180 union workers would be laid off. The Organizational Effectiveness unit and the local union leaders, cooperating in the hopes of avoiding the layoff, created what we call *Cost Study Teams* (CSTs). Six workers, their supervisor, and an engineer worked as a team during that 6-month period to find ways of cutting the Xerox production costs down to the level offered by the vendor. When this project was successful in the wire-harness department, the same framework was put into action in four other departments where vendor prices were threatening hundreds of jobs. When those CSTs came close enough to the savings target, their production and jobs were saved. Management estimates that the CST process saved up to 900 jobs.

As the company moved more aggressively to implement a *Competitive Benchmarking* program through all its production units, union and *Organizational Effectiveness* unit people found themselves in a bind between Employee Involvement and Competitive Benchmarking. To resolve this conflict, Harold Tragash, representing Organizational Effectiveness, formed an agreement with Norman Rickard, head of Competitive Benchmarking so that Employee Involvement and Competitive Benchmarking could work together.

Developing and implementing a new program of guidance for training workers and managers in participative management. Thomas Kayser, in charge of Organizational Effectiveness in the combined Engineering and Production Departments, had shown himself to be an effective trainer in the new approach. Since Xerox is a worldwide firm, no single individual or even no team of individuals could be expected to meet the worldwide need. Kayser built upon his training experiences to prepare a manual to guide training activities throughout the corporation. His book, *Mining Group Gold*, presents detailed suggestions and instructions regarding how the manager can develop effective group discussions so that subordinates and associates participate fully in the management process. *Mining Group Gold* has been translated into Japanese, French, Portuguese, and Spanish for use throughout Xerox.

In order to meet intensifying international competition, the case suggests that certain conditions for change must be met. Leadership must come from the top of the management organization, in setting a general direction. Then there must be personal ways of linking the corporate offices with the production plants. To maintain and encourage top management's interest in EI, the production people can devise ways of exhibiting what they have learned—and how this learning has helped reduce costs and develop now processes and products.

One of the most difficult problems in carrying out a major change is to discover how to deal with top management endorsed programs that conflict with each other at operating levels. The Organizational Effectiveness people and the union leaders worked out ways of recognizing impending conflicts and resolving them.

Finally, such broad and sweeping changes require greatly expanded training activities for the handling of technological innovations and for spreading EI through the various divisions of a company, at home and abroad.

The foregoing analysis suggests a general strategy. It does not produce a step-by-step set of procedures any organization can follow.

It does highlight the main problems to be resolved and indicates the strategies used by Xerox to resolve them. No organization can expect to follow the Xerox strategy in detail, but any comparable organization will have to develop its own strategies, adapted to its own conditions.

When other studies of such transformations have been made, we can compare the Xerox experience with these new cases, in the hope of arriving at the fundamental principles of structural and cultural transformation.

This seems a far cry from the neatness of the hypothesis testing approach, but that approach does not allow us to deal with far-reaching changes that follow social processes over many years.

The test of the effectiveness of this new approach will be determined by its *practical application*. That will not be determined in any single study, but the accumulation of other studies of structural and cultural transformation should lead us ahead to scientific generalizations based upon formal research processes and also on what skillful practitioners have learned from experience.

In the Xerox studies, I was beginning to learn how to go from the study of small, informal groups, to the study of large and complex industrial organizations. I was also learning how to go from theory to practice and from practice back to better theories of what works out in practice.

Note that what we have learned about the organizational changes of the 1980s and 1990s depends not only on the work of professional researchers but also on the reports by skillful practitioners. In the words of Donald Schon (1983), we need to collaborate with "reflective practitioners," people who not only have been deeply involved in organizational changes but who also have the capacity of generalizing from their own experience and the experience of their associates. For the social researcher identifying those skillful practitioners cannot be an exact science, but we can continually check their past reports against future experience. The conclusions we arrive at will never be so neat as those presented by hypothesis testing, but they will provide us with better guidance on how to turn research into practice.

This suggests the value of collaboration between professional social researchers and skillful practitioners in future applied sociology studies—a topic to which I turn later in the chapter on applied social research.

Finally, let me add some notes on strategies of case analysis. Do we proceed following a *deductive* strategy or an *inductive* strategy?

Those committed to hypothesis testing are implicitly following a deductive strategy. They assume that the problem area is already partly known in its general outlines, so the problem now is to fill in the blanks to aid them in moving from hypotheses to a theory which would best account for what they think they are finding out. That theory would not tell them what they need to do to gain a certain objective, but it would show how certain factors are more significant than others in influencing the problem area.

While I had never thought about it this way before, I now see that the research strategy I have followed is inductive. In starting a project in a field unfamiliar to me, I have begun by an open ended exploration. At first, the field seems full of confusion, but, through further interviewing and observation, I begin to see a rough pattern emerging. That pattern suggests a number of action alternatives to consider.

Before taking action or recommending that others take action, I scan the scene to discover other cases that appear to have similar elements. For example, in the Xerox case, I would compare it with other *large manufacturing companies heavily involved in international trade*. Did they face similar problems? If so, how did they go about solving them? If they arrived at similar solutions, that would strengthen my conviction that we were on the right track in discovering concrete solutions to major organizational problems.

If we find cases where they faced quite different problems or arrived at different solutions, that should force us to go back to rethink our strategies of case analysis and therefore our action strategies.

Taking this approach, there is no way we can be absolutely sure that the action alternative we propose is the best one for a particular case, but, in the early stages, what seemed to work in the first case studied is likely to be worth trying in other cases that seem similar. If that one is tried out and we can then examine what happened, that will enlarge our knowledge for future action alternatives.

CHAPTER THIRTEEN

METHODS FOR DOING APPLIED SOCIAL RESEARCH

My present commitment to *participatory action research* evolved of an early and continuing interest in the involvement of society's underdogs in participating in the decisions affecting them. In my first field studies in Boston's North End, I came to depend for collaboration on Ernest Pecci, a high school graduate, and Angelo Ralph Orlandella, a high school dropout. As I learned from them, people of relatively little formal education could nevertheless manifest a high level of intelligence and resourcefulness. Years later, in research with small farmers in Latin America, I came to the same conclusion with regard to people who had had much less formal education but nevertheless were demonstrating that they had practical knowledge about their farming methods that in some cases was more valid than what they were being told by professional experts.

These findings fitted in with my egalitarian orientation, developed early in life. Nevertheless, in my industrial and agricultural studies, I found innumerable cases where the industrial worker or the small farmer demonstrated practical knowledge beyond that of the highly educated professional. I did not conclude that higher education was useless but that it needed to be combined with what workers or farmers were learning from doing and thinking about their work.

In this line of thinking, I was not alone. I found myself participating in a broad social change involving the empowerment and participation of people in making the decisions affecting their livelihood. Those shared experiences led me to think of reshaping the social research process in such ways that some of those we studied participated in the research process.

That new strategy has been called *participatory action research* (PAR), or other names for the same phenomena by other people. Let us see how PAR arises from and departs from more established research methods.

Applied sociological research utilizes many of the methods used in nonapplied or basic research—for example, interviewing and observation, surveys, and documentary analysis. In applied sociological research, certain distinctive methods are built into the strategy of project organization.

I find it useful to distinguish between *policy research* and *action research*. In policy research, the sociologist follows what I call the *professional expert model*. The sociologist is called upon by the client organization (or gets himself or herself invited) to evaluate existing policies and to suggest policy changes to meet new objectives. In action research, the sociologist works with members of the organization for an extended period of time to help them to diagnose their problems and to develop social processes designed to improve organizational performance.

Until recently, the professional expert model was by far the strategy preferred by sociologists interested in applied research. It involved the minimum amount of change from basic research. Following the fieldwork he or she carried out or had done by assistants, the sociologist did not need to get involved with the organization beyond working out arrangements for the study with gatekeepers and reporting findings and recommendations to the organization's leaders. One hoped that the policy recommendations would be implemented and would yield good results, but the responsibility of the sociologist was discharged with presenting findings and recommendations.

For action research, we need first to clear up the existing confusion, in which various behavioral scientists have used action research, participatory research, and participatory action research interchangeably, as if all three terms referred to the same phenomena. I argue that there can be action research without participation and participatory research without action. In fact, until recently, most action research involved projects in which the professional researcher controlled the process of data gathering and application of research findings insofar as possible. There can also be participatory research without action objectives. In my *Street Corner Society* study, the men I called Doc and Sam Franco became, in a very real sense, coparticipant observers. We all hoped that publication of the book would eventually be helpful to the district and to others like it, but there were no specific action or policy recommendations. I suspect that this is quite common in social anthropological community or cultural studies. Certain individuals begin as informants, then become key informants, and end up as coparticipant observers, helping the professional fieldworker to interpret what they are learning from interviewing and observation.

PAR is a strategy in which one or more of the subject population participate in shaping the research design and data gathering and are also involved in the actions designed to follow. I did not invent PAR—in fact, there is considerable controversy regarding who first used the term. That controversy came to my attention in the Penn-Cornell conference on PAR. At that time, Cornell and University of Pennsylvania participants focused on PAR projects in which we had been involved.

We were attacked by a participant from another university, who claimed that we had misappropriated the term and had redefined it to apply only to Western European and U.S. *liberal* approaches to collaboration between management and labor or the university administration and the surrounding community. The critics argued that we had thereby excluded *revolutionary* cases in which the professional social researchers were trying to help the downtrodden people organize themselves to attack this domination.

In my 1991 book, I had defined PAR in the following words:

> In participatory action research (PAR), some of the people in the organization or community under study participate actively with the professional researcher throughout the research process from the initial design to the final presentation of results and discussion of action implications.

By the time of the Penn-Cornell conference on PAR in October, 1990, I had realized that this definition did not make clear what I had in mind. As it was then stated, it could include a project in which company management collaborated with a professional researcher to discover ways of undermining a union or a project in which the owner of a large Latin

American hacienda collaborated with a professional social researcher to find ways of keeping the peasants from organizing effectively.

That was not what I had in mind, and, in fact, none of the PAR projects I have studied have fit such a model where practitioner participation involves only members of management. This suggested an expansion of the definition to bring in the *values* I see in PAR. I would now add this sentence to the earlier definition:

> The social purpose underlying PAR is to empower low status people in the organization or community to make decisions and take actions which were previously foreclosed to them.

I hoped that expanded definition would be sufficient to bridge the gap between liberal and revolutionary PAR projects. If so, we don't need to argue over political ideologies and can get down to the applied social research business of discovering better ways of doing PAR.

Where it is possible to get the top-level people involved, a more thoroughgoing restructuring of social relations becomes possible than could happen without their participation. On the other hand, when it is not possible to engage top-level people in PAR projects, then it is appropriate to develop PAR as a means of organizing groups of low status people against the interests of top managers in industry or agriculture.

When and where did PAR projects get started? The first PAR case to come to my attention was The Sky River Project, carried out in the early 1970s by Timothy Kennedy. I was the chairman of his graduate committee when he wrote his doctoral thesis on that project (Kennedy, 1969).

As a Vista volunteer, Kennedy was sent to Alaska to work among the Eskimos. When his 2-year period was up, Kennedy extended his stay for 11 years to bring the project and related programs to completion.

At first, Kennedy needed to discover what role he could play to be most helpful to the Eskimo people in his village. He later defined three roles that an outsider might play: *power broker*, *liberal advocate*, and *facilitator*.

Although Eskimos are not American Indians, the local head of the Bureau of Indian Affairs in Kennedy's area of Alaska served as the principal power broker. Kennedy rejected that role as simply reenforcing the Eskimo's dependency on the white people.

After trying out the liberal advocate role, he rejected it as simply reenforcing the Eskimos dependence on other white people. If they followed his initiative in liberal advocacy, he would in effect become their leader, thus closing off the opportunities for leadership to arise among the Eskimos.

Kennedy discovered his role as facilitator through the use of videotaping technology. He was already familiar with videotaping and brought to the scene his own portable videotaping machine. So as to demistify a technology which was then new to the Eskimos, he demonstrated how to videotape and then invited some of the Eskimo people to try it out on any scenes they wanted to portray.

Then Kennedy suggested that this technology might give them the opportunity to focus on their problems in such a way that they could have an impact on the white authorities. Discussion revealed three major problems:

1. There was no regional high school serving the widely scattered villages. For the school year, the Eskimo high school students were sent away by plane to Indian schools in Oregon and Oklahoma. When they came back, they no longer fitted into Eskimo culture nor did they fit into the white culture.
2. The houses built for the Eskimos by the federal government were not properly insulated, and the floors were sagging.
3. The electric power to the villages had broken down when the power lines were buried under the permafrost earth, as had been specified by the federal Rural Electrification Administration.

The focus on each problem was developed through group discussions, which were videotaped. The villagers were asked to select a principal spokesperson for each problem, and that person was interviewed on videotape by Kennedy, with his Eskimo assistant. As the program further developed, Eskimos took over the interviewing and taping.

For the spokesperson, Kennedy asked him to determine where and how he wished to be interviewed. For example, for the high school problem, William Trader wanted to be interviewed in his own back yard, while he was repairing a fish net.

The spokesperson was the first villager to view the videotape. At that time, he could decide to accept it as it was or else introduce changes. Then that videotape was shown to the villagers, who had the right to accept it as representing their views or to introduce changes.

Before the videotapes were shown to outsiders, Kennedy required the villagers to sign their names to a statement that the tape represented their views. He wanted to emphasize to authorities that this was not a videotape documentary produced by film professionals but was authentically their own production.

Kennedy provided background information regarding the bureaucratic agencies and officials they might want to see a particular videotape. When they had decided what they wanted to do, Kennedy and his Eskimo assistant went to the agency offices and arranged for the chief administrator to view the film.

He then offered the official the opportunity to send a videotaped reply to the community. So as to make clear that he was not trying to put officials on the spot, he offered them the same rights that he had given the Eskimos. Before the interview tape was sent back to the community, the official viewed it himself and, if he wished, he had the right to revise his remarks.

This strategy had some striking results in creating changes in governmental policies and building up a sense of self esteem in the original village and in stimulating other villages to get themselves organized in similar ways.

The videotape on the school problem was only 15 minutes long, but it had a powerful impact. William Trader told them what the high school policy did to disrupt families and disorient students. The final scene showed the high school students at the village airport, saying their tearful goodbyes, and then taking off in the plane, while their parents stood silently watching them go.

The educational authorities had never heard any Eskimo complaints about the policy of sending the high school students to Indian schools in Oregon and Oklahoma. They had considered building regional high schools, but had rejected such a policy as too costly. Now the initial showing of the tape to education officials reopened the question and led directly to a $149 million program to build regional high schools for the scattered Eskimo villages in various areas.

The frequent breakdowns of electric power in 35 of their villages had brought Eskimo complaints to the Rural Electrification Administration (REA) and to the Alaskan Village Electrification Cooperative (AVEC). Those had all been referred to Washington headquarters of the REA, where they had been referred to officials who had originally insisted that the cables be laid underground, and the complaints were ignored.

The head of AVEC viewed the showing in which Eskimos stood on two sides of a large crevasse created by permafrost, which had ruptured the cable, and argued for a different plan. He was convinced, but he needed the videotape to take to Washington to show it to the top REA officials. This led to abandonment of the old plan and acceptance of Eskimo suggestions to string overhead wires to homes and have them powered by oil-fired generators.

The problems of the government-built houses had been referred to the housing department engineers, who had had them built. The engineers ruled that the houses were well insulated and that no floors deviated more than a quarter inch from level. The videotape showed the interior of an Eskimo house, with ice forming on the walls. On the floor, an Eskimo provided a child's kaleidoscope, which he set at one wall and then let it go, whereupon it rolled down to the middle of the floor and beyond it. The camera followed the kaleidoscope as it rolled back and forth.

When this tape was shown to the board of directors of the Eskimo housing program, it provoked a heated argument. When the executive of the program still refused to acknowledge the legitimacy of the complaints, the board discharged him and appointed a new director to act on the Eskimo complaints.

As the Sky River Project extended beyond the original village, with showings of the tapes in other villages, the Eskimos realized for the first time that they shared the complaints and problems of the original village. The villages were so far apart geographically that they were not aware they had so much in common. This led to a sense of empowerment in the villages, so that now, in meetings with authorities, the Eskimos pressed their suggestions more vigorously.

Eskimo villagers in Alaska are strongly egalitarian and are accustomed to work out problems among themselves through group discussions, arriving at a consensus. Any individual who appears to be more aggressive in seeking leadership is not respected.

When state and federal authorities visited one of the scattered small villages, they would call a community meeting to learn about the problems people were facing. A man who had worked for a white village power broker would step forward to present his views. The authorities would therefore assume he was the village leader. In their own language, the Eskimos called this person a *playboss*.

Through the Sky River Project, the authorities recognized that they were now getting the authentic voice of the people, through their chosen spokesperson and through all the signatures of the people authorizing their village communication.

The project was exceptional among other PAR projects in the use of modern videotape technology to facilitate effective discussion and action programs across ethnic and status and bureaucratic rankings of officials (Whyte, 1984).

At the time when the Sky River Project was going on, I learned about the Norwegian shipping project, carried out in the 1960s under the direction of social psychologist Einar Thorsrud (1977). He simply called it part of the Industrial Democracy Project, but in every respect it fits the definition of PAR. In this project, Thorsrud and his behavioral science associates worked with representatives of government, the shipping companies, ship officers and crew and union officers to redesign the physical structure and the social and technological systems of merchant marine ships to improve the quality of work life and to reduce the size of crews so as to make Norwegian ships more cost-competitive with fleets paying lower wages. The project not only transformed Norway's merchant marine but also had a worldwide impact, giving rise to similar changes in other countries.

With coauthors, I have reported on more recent cases in industry, agricultural research and development, and in urban revitalization. The cases involve Xerox and the Mondragón cooperatives in industry, cases in Latin American agriculture, and the program of the University of Pennsylvania in collaboration with people and institutions in the depressed urban area surrounding the university. (Whyte, ed. 1990; Greenwood, Whyte, & Harkavy, 1993).

As I reviewed those previous cases, it occurred to me to rethink my *Street Corner Society* study, calling it then participatory research, since I did not originally plan on actions coming out of the research. In fact, several major actions did arise out of my North End Activities. I had prevailed upon the director of a settlement house to hire Ernest Pecci (Doc) as the director of one of the three storefront recreation centers for corner boys and young men. The other two centers were directed by men from outside with Masters' degrees in social work. Within 2 weeks of the opening of the social workers centers, they had to be shut down, as the directors were unable to maintain order. Pecci's center ran smoothly from the first day until the end of the grant funds supporting the centers, thus confirming my judgment that an older corner-boy leader would be more effective with the boys 12- to 19-years-old.

With the leadership of Angelo Ralph Orlandella and Ernest Pecci, I organized a protest march on City Hall to protest the lack of hot water in the public bathhouse, erratic garbage collections, and other evidences of neglect of this district. This project produced some immediate results in the bathhouse and some temporary improvements in other city services.

After I left the district, Orlandella pulled together the leadership of all of the corner gangs that had participated in the protest march to form a softball league. For this, they needed a field on which to play. The corner gangs, joined by younger boys, worked for several weeks clearing the debris from the old gas house lot to make it available for softball. When neighbors complained that home runs went out of the lot onto their buildings, the police banned softball on this site. Working through the settlement house director and a North End politician who was serving on the Mayor's staff, Orlandella got a Parks Department appropriation for a wire fence high enough to block the home runs. The softball league then carried through a full summer schedule, with wide community interest.

When Orlandella enlisted in the Marine Corps at the start of World War II, that ended his community work in the North End. In his subsequent career, he used his native talents for social observation with what he learned in working with me on spotting group leadership outside of his home community, and he carried on his own informal experiments in the Marine Corps, in the Air Force, and later, upon his retirement, as superintendent of Public Works in the town of Burlington, outside of Boston. The seven superintendents before Orlandella has served only a year, more or less; Ralph served for 7 years and then voluntarily retired.

With these action spin-offs, should *Street Corner Society* be reclassified as PAR? If so, would that make it the earliest PAR project on record? That would be a foolish claim. As noted earlier, many social anthropological projects have involved collaboration from indigenous people, and reviewing the whole record would reveal other cases before mine where participatory research evolved into PAR. The question now should not be one of establishing priority but rather learning how to explore the PAR possibilities and limitations so that we can improve our research and practice.

--------------------◆◆◆--------------------

If the applied sociologist is interested in working on major social and technical changes in industrial, agricultural, and community organizations, then it seems to me that PAR is the most promising strategy. The *professional expert role* of just reporting what the research says that organizational leaders should do is not likely to be helpful for a complex process of change that is bound to last many months.

Without participation of the subjects of study, the consultant in *action research* runs into serious dilemmas. If he or she is to serve the change process effectively, there must be a continuing involvement with the parties for an extended period of time. If the consultant does not have a long-range contract, then there is the temptation to try to extend the consulting period—with concerns over whether this is dictated by the needs of the client or the financial interests of the consultant. Consultants generally claim to believe that their primary mission is to help clients so effectively that they will no longer need outside assistance—but that objective conflicts with the financial interests of the consultant. Furthermore, when that objective is achieved, the consultant may lose not only continuing contracts but also vital research information regarding further developments within the client organization.

PAR avoids such dilemmas and also offers positive strengths not available through action research *without participation*. The social researcher needs to gain some understanding of the technical side of operations performed by the organization. Without internal assistance, the researcher tries to pick up enough information from reading and interviewing to gain some understanding of the technical processes, but the knowledge so gained can be no more than superficial. If one of the insider PAR collaborators is technically trained, that can be an important safeguard against faulty interpretations. The social researcher's need to gain an understanding of the culture of the organization can, to some extent, be picked up in the course of the study, but there will be many subtle aspects that can be learned only through very long periods of fieldwork. Whether or not the insider PAR participant is technically trained, he or she can be an important source of information on the culture of the organization.

Rarely if ever does a significant scientific discovery become applied in practice immediately following the announcement of the achievement. The path from discovery to practical application goes through a research and development (R&D) process, which may involve a substantial investment in the time and talents of applied researchers and technicians. Sociology provides neither the traditions nor the organizational structures for the R&D process. In moving from research into application, the sociologist needs the help of insiders who have been involved in the research process. When the social researcher and the insider PAR participants work together to guide the transition between research and practice, they can help to create an effective R&D process. The insider PAR participant now has a personal stake and can be counted on to interpret the basic ideas and defend them to other organization members. In studies of major organizational changes, researchers have always found one or more "champions" of the new ideas. They have been placed strategically but not in positions where they could simply give orders to implement the changes. They were respected enough so that others listened to them, and they were strongly enough committed to continue to advocate the changes in spite of some resistance.

In the standard research process, the professional researcher tries to exercise as much control as possible over the research design, data gathering, and reporting of findings. In PAR, control is shared jointly between the professional researchers and the practitioners. This means that PAR is not appropriate if the main purpose is to test a particular hypothesis—unless the insider PAR participants can be persuaded that the proposed research operations will also lead to practical results for the organization.

On the other hand, PAR opens up the possibility of achieving what I call "creative surprises" (Whyte, 1989). In the first Xerox project, we found a new framework for interpreting the relationship between participation and productivity and for understanding the ways in which allocation of overhead or indirect costs can distort measurements of worker productivity. I had always assumed that the industrial accounting figures management used reflected organizational reality—unless some managers falsified the data. As the workers challenged the overhead costs allocated to their department, I saw that such allocations were often set in ways which exaggerated labor costs and thus added to the apparent cost of labor. That did not tell me how to do industrial accounting myself, but it told me the first question to ask management: "How do you allocate your overhead costs?"

This analysis provoked me to rethink the relationship between participation and productivity. A long list of previous studies had failed to find a consistent relationship between participation and productivity —workers liked to participate, but that did not always yield higher productivity.

I reasoned that there was something wrong with conventional ways of measuring worker productivity. In many organizations, workers take on tasks earlier performed by supervisors. We could thus have a situation where the workers are producing as much output as before and yet the number of management people has been sharply reduced. It makes no sense to say that productivity has been unchanged while the operation has become more efficient.

I now conclude that productivity depends on the total contributions of people and the resources used. Economists call this *total factor productivity*. Each of those factors costs money so a measurement of the factor costs will yield better measures of productivity. On that basis, I would expect that future studies would show a consistent positive relationship between participation and productivity.

This "creative surprise" led me to rethink and replan future studies of industrial productivity that I—or anyone else—might undertake in the future. I now know much better than before how to avoid past mistakes in such productivity and participation studies.

In the FAGOR project in the Mondragón cooperatives, Davydd Greenwood and his insider PAR participants developed a new framework for interpreting organizational culture. They found widespread agreement on the basic values of the cooperatives but considerable disagreement and debate about how to realize those values in practice.

The Xerox and FAGOR projects produced "creative surprises" in that they could not have happened in a conventional research project. They arose out of PAR as we and the practitioners worked together to solve practical organizational problems.

A major key to the success of a PAR project is the ability of the professional researcher to identify one or more *reflective practitioners*—people who not only have had experience with the problem area but also have been thinking creatively about the culture and social systems of their organization. When the professional social researcher and the practitioner(s) get together to explore their common interests, they can then go on to discuss concretely how they will jointly work out the research design and how practitioners will participate in data gathering and analysis, and how concrete actions might arise out of the research findings.

With more experience in this relatively new field of PAR, professional behavioral scientists can work out in greater detail various possible PAR models and develop guidelines that would be helpful to the parties considering organizing a PAR project.

While this is still a relatively new field, PAR is now being pursued by feminist sociologists and by students of agricultural and industrial research and development all over the world. It is clear that PAR is becoming a major applied research strategy in the world of economic and social development studies.

CHAPTER FOURTEEN
COMBINING CONSULTING AND APPLIED SOCIAL RESEARCH

There are time and financial barriers to overcome in doing field research and in moving from fieldwork to publication. If consulting is intended to be combined with research, the time requirements for each function are likely to interfere with each other. The consultant must be prepared to fit his or her schedule to the needs of the client. It often happens that a need for consulting is communicated to the consultant by the client organization, which then needs attention at a particular time. If such time demands cannot be met, the consultancy relationship may lapse. Therefore, in order to keep the consultancy function viable, the professor often must put aside other assignments—and further research and especially the writing and rewriting research reports tend to be postponed and eventually be dropped.

Can consulting be combined with social research and development? It is not easy but some individuals have done it successfully. Beyond individual contributions, can it be institutionalized on a group basis? If so, can that institutionalization arise within a university?

My one experience with trying to build a program around this combination arose in the early 1980s in the ILR Extension Division, where I worked after my formal retirement in 1979. Donald Kane, Director of State Wide Management Programs, had arranged to bring Xerox personnel officials and their union leaders to Cornell for a week of off-site training and discussion. Peter Lazes was then serving as the outside consultant to the Xerox program.

Discussions with Don and Peter suggested that something very unusual was going on at Xerox. We felt that it was important to bring this type of program within the Extension Division of the ILR School. Peter was interested in an academic position. Extension Division Director Lois Gray wanted to help bring this about, but she had no funds to support a professorial appointment for Peter. Nevertheless, we proceeded to create the Programs for Employment and Workplace Systems (PEWS) in the ILR Extension Division, with three codirectors: Don, Peter, and me.

I had been leading a group of several professors in studying cases where employees, about to lose their jobs through a plant shutdown, combined to buy the plant and save their jobs—at least temporarily. When Steven Allinger, staff assistant to the Assembly Committee on Higher Education, learned about the coming shutdown of Bethlehem Steel operations in Lackawanna, near Buffalo, he was especially concerned since he had grown up in a town near Lackawanna and felt some commitment to that area—even though it had nothing to do with his Assembly job duties.

Looking for someone in New York State who was doing research on employee buyouts, through a roundabout set of coincidences, Allinger got in touch with me. At the time, I was supervising a Ph.D. thesis for Edwin (Wynn) Houser on the Hyatt-Clark Industries buyout of an old General Motors plant.

Allinger arranged to have Wynn and me fly to Albany to discuss employee ownership and worker buyouts with him and other Assembly staff members. Steve followed up that meeting by coming to Cornell to meet with Director Lois Gray, Don Kane, Wynn Houser, and me.

By this time, my inquiries with specialists on the steel industry had made it clear that an employee buyout of the Lackawanna works was out of the question. For more than 40 years, Bethlehem had not invested any money in modernizing the plants, so massive sums would be needed to purchase and modernize the facilities.

Steve accepted this conclusion, but that did not stop him. The State was often called upon for emergency help when a major shutdown occurred, he said, but, would it not be better if the State had some way of anticipating such disasters so that preventive measures could be undertaken? We agreed and Steve went back to Albany to draft a bill providing $200,000 for the first year of support for PEWS.

That bill was introduced into the Assembly too late to be acted upon in the current academic year, but, in the following year it was included in

Governor Cuomo's budget proposal, and it passed into law. Here we probably had strong backing from Lieutenant Governor Stan Lundine. Before he was elected to Congress, Lundine had been Mayor of Jamestown, where he was known particularly for his role in creating the Jamestown Area Labor-Management Committee (JALMC) for work on industrial development. I had been involved in studies of the work of JALMC. Later, when I became involved with Congress in promoting employee ownership, Lundine, Matthew F. McHugh of Ithaca, and Peter Kostmayer of Bucks County, Pennsylvania, introduced to Congress the "The Voluntary Job Preservation and Community Stabilization Act" (H.R. 12870, May 25, 1978). That bill never passed into law, but it stirred up a lot of interest in Congress, especially through the work of Joseph Blasi, social policy advisor to Kostmayer, and Corey Rosen, assistant to Senator Gaylord Nelson on the Senate Select Committee on Small Business. (Both went on to pursue careers focusing on employee ownership. Rosen created The National Center for Employee Ownership, whose newsletters have become the primary source for information and ideas on current developments in this field. Blasi has become a leading producer of employee ownership research.)

Beyond my community interests, I wanted to build PEWS for two interrelated purposes:

1. To establish applied social research as a legitimate and important objective for professors of industrial and labor relations. Up to this time, there were several members of the teaching faculty who were interested in applied research, but the predominant mode was for professors to engage in what they called *basic* research—and they tended to look down on applied researchers. I wanted to demonstrate that a given project could be *applied* and *basic* at the same time: applied in dealing with practical problems and basic in yielding advances in theory and knowledge.

2. I wanted to break down the barriers between Extension and the resident faculty by getting some PEWS people involved in teaching undergraduate and graduate courses. In the early years of the School, there were several joint appointments between Extension and the resident faculty, so Extension people were in effect teaching on-campus courses. Later the resident faculty had voted to block any future joint

appointments. I thought that was unfortunate; if there were more interchange between Extension and the resident faculty, we could all learn from each other.

The $200,000 state grant for PEWS secured an ILR faculty position for Peter. Beyond that, we had an understanding that PEWS could charge for our services. That enabled us to provide some services free to clients who could not afford to pay but charge top rates for private companies and lesser rates to unions, schools, and hospitals. Overall, we found that we were able to more than double the state funds, greatly expanding our capacity to serve projects—and, we hoped, leaving money free to support research, growing out of a field project, when the client organization was not prepared to provide research support.

In the early stages, we had a professional staff of six and two secretaries. Five of the six professionals were involved in field projects; I was no longer able to undertake fieldwork, but I continued active in consulting with my colleagues, demoting myself from codirector to research director.

I teamed up with Michael Gaffney to propose a course on "Cooperative Strategies for Strengthening Organizational Performance" (ILR 675). Both in terms of field experience and education, Mike was highly qualified. He had a B.S. degree in nautical science from the U.S. Merchant Marine Academy and was a licensed officer and pilot for ocean and Great Lakes shipping. He also had a Ph.D. from Ohio State in anthropology and had published some of his research.

To offer this course to undergraduates and graduate students, we had to have the approval of the Department of Organizational Behavior, in which I was now an inactive member. After all my years of teaching in that department, they could not turn us down.

For 2 years, Mike and I taught the course together, using case studies from the literature and from our own and PEWS experience in current fieldwork. Student interest ran high, and some of the faculty members were impressed with what they heard of the course. For the third year of ILR 675, we proposed that Mike teach the course alone, and that breakthrough was accepted.

The next opening came later when PEWS had hired Frank Wayno, who had a B.S. degree in engineering from Cornell and a Ph.D. degree from Princeton in sociology. The College of Engineering, pressed by its alumni, had committed itself to developing a master's degree in manufacturing. For that, they needed an introductory course in organizational behavior. Frank adapted ILR 675 for the College of Engineering, while Mike continued to teach ILR 675.

This ILR innovation in the Engineering College went so well that an engineering professor invited Frank to coteach with him a course on Project Management. This brought the PEWS contribution to three courses and helped to overcome the barriers against extension participation in on-campus teaching.

The College of Engineering and the Johnson Graduate School of Business had established a joint masters degree in engineering and business administration. The ILR and PEWS innovations suggested the idea of including ILR students in the masters program in manufacturing. To further develop these intercollege relationships, Frank Wayno worked with professor Albert George, head of COMEPP, the Cornell Management and Engineering Productivity Program, in establishing the Center for Manufacturing Enterprise (CME). With George as Director and Wayno as Executive Director, CME was approved by the University Board of Trustees in January 1994.

CME aims to provide consulting and applied research services to manufacturing companies, and it stimulated the development in the School of Business of a manufacturing semester, in which students spent all of their study time on various aspects of manufacturing, guided by professors in that school and in ILR and the Engineering College.

PEWS has played a major role in developing these intercollege research and teaching relations.

To guide PEWS in the development of an applied research program, we established an academic advisory committee on research. We invited as members professors who were sympathetic with applied research but also were strategically placed and highly respected in their own departments: one from each of the four major ILR departments, plus a professor of business administration, a professor from the Department of City and Regional Planning in the College of Architecture, Art and Planning and a professor from the College of Engineering.

The first major publication of PEWS arose out of our previous research with Xerox and the ACTWU in their development of Cost Study Teams to save jobs. We had then expanded that approach to cover two other companies, who had tried the same strategy in efforts to avoid plant or departmental shutdowns. *A Fighting Chance* by Sally Klingel and Ann Martin was published by the ILR Press in 1989.

Building further on our past research with Xerox, at the suggestion of a member of the Academic Advisory group, we undertook a study of the transformation of Xerox over a period of more than a decade. This project was based on interviews by Frank Wayno of the principal actors in this transformation in the divisions of manufacturing, engineering, marketing, and servicing organizations. That provided the Xerox information and ideas described in Chapter 12.

In the same period, Mike Gaffney and Sally Klingel carried on research on mutual gains (or interest) bargaining, Ann Martin has been developing a program of studies of reform movements in public schools, and Edward Cohen-Rosenthal led a group in applied research on industrial and community ecology programs.

As every professor active in research soon learns in seeking support from foundations or government agencies, the funding agency is inclined to provide support for salaries and expenses in fieldwork but only allows a minimum of time for writing research reports. We often find that the essential ideas to be communicated are not readily apparent, and, in fact, some of the best published articles are written long after the end of fieldwork, when the professor has had time for further reflection and rethinking. For a professor in the regular on-campus teaching program, the lapse between the end of fieldwork and the writing of one's best contribution need not be a large problem. The professor can continue to reflect and rethink and rewrite research publications long after grant support has ended, while continuing on the regular salary provided by the university or college. Some of my best publications have come out months or years after the completion of the fieldwork.

The situation is quite different for the PEWSian, who seeks to combine consulting and applied research. Since our salaries are financed only partially by the State, each PEWSian engaged in fieldwork incurs an obligation to bring in a quota of contract funds. Most of our industrial clients are not interested in providing funds to cover research, beyond our regular consulting fees. Support therefore must be sought elsewhere.

I attempted to fill this financial gap by applying to various foundations for support of the applied research that arose out of our consulting activities. Over the years, I had been reasonably successful in raising grant money to cover my own research—always emphasizing the *basic* nature of what I had in mind, while I continued to pursue *applied* ends. For the program grant for PEWS, I was unsuccessful.

Thus, if we wanted to pursue applied research further, we would have to somehow "bootleg" it into existing projects or seek support for a particular project, rather then a general program grant.

The project for the *A Fighting Chance* research was supported by a $12,000 grant from the New York State Center for Employee Ownership and Participation. When we totaled up the cost of the project, including partial salaries for several months for coauthors Klingle and Martin and field expenses, we figured that the cost of the project to PEWS was about 3 times the amount of the subsidy.

The much more ambitious project for the study of the transformation of the Xerox corporation was supported by a grant of $20,000 from CAHRS, the Center for Advanced Human Resources studies in the ILR Department of Personnel and Human Resources. (CAHRS is supported by $10,000 annual grants from companies to support personnel relevant research.) The main item of expense was the partial support of Frank Wayno's salary for several months of fieldwork and report writing. The Wayno report was delayed beyond the time projected because the writing and rewriting took longer than had been projected. Here again we estimated that the total cost for PEWS was about 3 times as much as the subsidy.

This means that PEWS has to make enough income on consulting contracts to cover the gap between research contract income and expenses—beyond the annual amount that PEWS has been expected to contribute to the ILR Extension budget, a sum which keeps expanding as State support for higher education declines.

To cover the gap between expenses and grant income, PEWS faces more problems than those faced by professors on regular annual salaries for teaching and research. In such cases, the professor may budget a month or two of expenses for submitting the final report to the funding agency. We may know that the write-up time budgeted is insufficient, but we also know from experience that funding agencies are much more willing to provide funds for fieldwork and data analysis than for report writing. Therefore, the tendency is to underestimate the writing time to be budgeted. This generally means that the final report reaches the funding agency several months later than promised. And then some months or a year or so may pass between the final report to the funding agency and the publication of articles or a book out of the research.

As long as the professor develops a reputation of doing good work and getting it published, funding agencies don't seem to worry about the delays. Nor does the professor worry that he or she or the organizational unit will suffer because the salaries of tenured professors continue without penalties on them or their organization. (The nontenured professor, of course, is under much greater pressure to get the writing and publication done.)

The PEWSian does not have this "safety net" on his or her salary. In the annual budget planning, PEWS people meet to figure out how much each one of us will earn to cover the gap between promised salaries and regular financial support from the state budget. If the individual's contract earnings fall short of what he or she projected at the start of the year, that does not affect that individual's salary, but no PEWSian wants to shift some of his or her financial burden to other members.

Can PEWS generate income through on-campus teaching? When we began with ILR 675, we were happy to contribute that teaching to the ILR School as a means of gaining an entry to on-campus teaching. We earned goodwill from the ILR department of Organizational Behavior and from Dean Lipsky and Associate Dean for Extension, Seeber. The good reputation that PEWS enjoyed with the state government helped the ILR school in its annual negotiations with SUNY and the State government, but it did not give us any immediate income.

The courses Wayno was teaching in the Engineering College do yield income to the ILR School, and some of that income goes to cover Wayno's salaries.

We are happy with this expansion of PEWS activities, but it does bring with it new responsibilities. Wayno's activities with the Engineering College have led directly to the creation of the Center for Manufacturing Enterprise (CME) linking Cornell units together and especially the Engineering College, the Johnson Graduate School of Business Administration, and the ILR School around teaching and applied research in manufacturing. When Wayno was appointed Executive Director of CME, part of his salary in the PEWS budget was supported by Dean Lipsky.

That takes care of Wayno's commitments to PEWS for salary, but here Frank has encountered a typical university problem: the professor who proves himself resourceful and has been successful in mobilizing others to action now finds himself overloaded with entrepreneurial and administrative functions.

This focus on the financial and organizational problems of PEWS should not overshadow the net gains we have made in the course of 12 years since we began.

In the beginning, PEWS was looked upon with some suspicion within the overall Extension Program. We were organized and operated quite differently than the district Extension programs. Some professors in the resident teaching and research programs were advising graduate students that working with PEWS would endanger their chances for good academic careers.

By 1996, the situation is quite different. PEWS is collaborating with Extension district offices on various programs, and we are finding that we are learning from each other. In resident instruction, professors are now inclined to foster their graduate students working with PEWS. The student gains far greater access to industrial research sites through PEWS than would be available otherwise, and it is now recognized that some of the best doctoral theses are being written by students working with PEWS.

We are now beginning to see active collaboration in research between PEWS and professors in the resident program, combining the intimate field knowledge of the PEWSian with the more comprehensive knowledge of the academic research literature of the professor in the resident program.

CHAPTER FIFTEEN

A VISION FOR SOCIOLOGY AND SOCIETY

What have I learned about individuals, groups, organizations and communities that might be useful for the further development of sociology (or of the behavioral sciences more generally)? And what have I learned that might be useful for solving the social and economic problems of American society? Much of what I learned came out of my fieldwork or that of my students or associates.

In the 1940s I became interested in studying the rare cases I found of union-management cooperation—at the time when most of my colleagues were studying conflict. Off and on, through the years I have searched for the bases of cooperation in industrial relations and then also within other spheres of society. That led to my focus on joint-payoff relations, especially when they were linked with multi-objective program planning, which widens the range of topics for cooperation.

I have long been interested in discovering ways that low-status people in organizations and communities can increase their impact on events. That calls for finding ways that such people can participate effectively.

As I focused on social structures and processes over the years, I found socially creative individuals who were able to move their communities or organizations in new and productive pathways. As I studied them, I found them creating social inventions that shaped and guided them and their associates along new and more rewarding pathways. I wanted to learn more about the possibilities of such social inventions.

A single individual can make an enormous difference in what happens in communities and organizations. Here I am not simply referring to the impact of someone who gets to the top of an organization or who is elected to the top position in a political structure. In many cases, such an individual just continues business or politics as usual, without any broad or lasting impact on his fellow citizens. I am interested rather in the cases of the leader who creates social changes that have reshaped communities and organizations in democratic and participatory ways.

The most striking cases I have encountered have been in markedly different social and economic settings: the peasant village of Huayopampa in Peru, an Eskimo community in Alaska, the Mondragón workers' cooperative complex in the Basque country of Spain, and the participatory action research program of the University of Pennsylvania.

In each case, I write of a leader who had a vision, but I must qualify that term to meet the objection of Davydd J. Greenwood who writes, "I know people who have wonderful, creative, and important visions and whose behavior ensures that nothing will be done or that they will be resisted actively."

The *visionary* leaders I have in mind not only had important ideas but also the capacity to stimulate others to act creatively and participate fully in the processes of democratic change. This meant not only signaling the general direction of change but also creating social inventions to change the social structures and to shape the social processes of discussion and action.

In the village of Huayopampa (see Chapter 10), Ceferino Villars, the school director provided the initial vision and restructured the school curriculum, and changed teacher-pupil relations so that pupils were involved in the upkeep of the school and in the work of the experimental gardens. Villars and his sons who followed him as teachers in Huayopampa got the villagers in touch with the Agrarian University to lead the village into raising tropical fruits. They worked with pupils and their parents to develop cooperative enterprises.

In the case of the Sky River Project in Alaska (see Chapter 13), the visionary leader was Timothy Kennedy, who came into the village first as a Vista Volunteer and then remained for a total of 11 years, becoming closely integrated into the community. Kennedy guided the villagers toward the development of a highly successful fishing and fish processing cooperative, organized along unorthodox lines to fit with the local culture. He introduced them to videotaping technology and guided them in using it participatively within their community and then in communicating ever more persuasively with the white authorities.

In the Mondragón case (see Chapter 11), Don José María Arizmendiarrieta provided the initial vision and organizing drive behind it. He created an essential series of social inventions and shaped the continuing dialogue with his associates. He led the way to the development of an extraordinarily able group of men and women to lead and expand the cooperative complex.

I have referred to the Penn case in Chapter 12, but it deserves fuller treatment now than the others because the Penn experience is probably most relevant for American experience.

In these cases, education played an essential role in the transformation of their communities. But note that this was not simply more of the usual education that had been practiced in their communities. In Huayopampa, the Villars shifted education away from rote learning toward a focus on the ecology and the culture of the indigenous community, and organized the school in terms of cooperative work teams for building maintenance and for cultivating the school farm plots.

In Mondragón, Don José María carried on seminars for discussion of social and economic problems, leading to the commitment of his first disciples to founding the first worker cooperative. Even as Ulgor got under way, Don José María met with the original workers after the work day to discuss and study with them how to structure the first worker cooperative—along the lines that later shaped the development of all the cooperatives in the complex. In this process, he also established the custom of study and reflective discussion that came to permeate the social processes of governance and work group collaboration that have been mainstays in the building of the cooperative complex.

In the Penn case, the social changes were brought about with and through a major university—which partially reshaped itself in the course of carrying out the new program.

The visionary leaders of the University of Pennsylvania program have been three American historians, Sheldon Hackney, Ira Harkavy, and Lee Benson. When Sheldon Hackney became president of the university, he found himself leading an institution that had built up an adversarial relationship with the surrounding community, as the university had been expanding at the expense of its slum neighbors. Hackney resolved to improve relations with the surrounding neighborhoods through a collaborative and participative program in which administrators, professors, and students worked with local institutions to do applied social research on social and economic problems and to enable the West Philadelphia people and the University to solve some of those problems.

Ira Harkavy and Lee Benson worked to establish the structures and social processes to make this collaboration possible. The University worked with neighborhood leaders to establish the West Philadelphia Improvement Corps (WEPIC), and Harkavy and Benson established a local base of activities in the Turner Middle School. This was the first step of setting up a three-cornered relationship: the university, the school, and the neighborhood. Later the university also established collaborative relationships with three middle schools, two neighborhood high schools, and two elementary schools.

These relationships were originally sponsored by the Penn Program for Public Service and are now centered in the Center for Community Partnerships, which is designed to involve alumni, faculty, and graduate and undergraduate students in working with WEPIC on the social, economic, and health problems of West Philadelphia.

They are supported by the broad-based Greater Philadelphia Urban Affairs Coalition and the Philadelphia School District. Other agencies involved have been unions, job training agencies, churches, and city, state, and federal officials and departments.

WEPIC's most intensive involvement has been with the Turner Middle School. In the academic year 1993–94, over 260 Penn faculty, staff, and students participated in programs in that school. The Turner program is the most fully developed and serves as a pilot program for the entire effort.

The Turner program does not stop at the end of a school day or at the end of a school year. Penn faculty and students have been involved in Saturday morning and Wednesday evening classes. The summer program has concentrated on strategies for revitalizing communities through working with the schools.

The program has had a marked effect on curriculum planning at the University. Courses in Anthropology, History, Nursing, and Education have been developed around Penn faculty and student involvement in the Turner Middle School. Other Penn courses have been developed or adapted for working with other schools. A growing number of masters and Ph.D. theses has grown out of this community involvement.

This new form of outreach is supported by small financial incentives to professors for designing new courses to focus on the problems of West Philadelphia or to redesign an existing course so as to include fieldwork with WEPIC. Some students also get small work-study grants for working with the program. This support is in line with what is available in other universities for professors for teaching summer school courses and for students on research assistantships or work-study programs.

This program has no assigned staff but is based on the appeal of linking teaching, research of faculty, and research of undergraduate students in working with WEPIC.

The various health-related activities have stirred the interest of many pupils in pursuing health careers—from nurses aides, to nurses, to technicians, and to doctors. This is a field where employment is growing, so pupils are being guided to where the jobs will be.

The program has had a major impact upon race relations in the University as black and white professors work together on the common problems they are studying. In some cases, where there are team projects, black and white students work on the same teams.

When the university shut down a fraternity house on campus, Harkavy arranged for it to be taken over as a residence for black and white students working with WEPIC. That further strengthens the working and social relations among ethnic groups.

Why do students get involved with WEPIC? An important motive is undoubtedly altruism on the part of black and white middle-class students, but in this case altruism is rewarded with exciting educational experiences in working together on studying and trying to solve some of the problems of the neighborhood. This experience also opens up new opportunities for career development related to social service and health activities. Instead of an activity separate from academic work, the Penn program provides a basis for bachelors or masters or doctoral degrees. It does not depend only on altruism.

The program has involved an extraordinarily large number of Penn professors and students in working with and through WEPIC—and that number grows from year to year. It has attracted wide attention especially from other urban universities. This has been stimulated by a grant from the Dewitt Wallace Readers Digest Fund to support the adaptation of the

Penn program in two or more other universities. That grant also supports the publication and circulation of the Penn quarterly publication on universities, schools, and communities. That quarterly has helped to stimulate and guide other universities through reporting on the Penn program and on others in cities where efforts are being made to build on the Penn model for their own urban outreach programs.

The university is being reshaped and reoriented in line with a vision first proposed by President Sheldon Hackney and now strongly supported by his successor, President Judith Rodin. That vision has unleashed a growing flow of initiatives on the part of deans, department chairs, and professors to develop new and exciting ways to link university education with the solving of community problems—in participatory ways.

A small shift in the university's resources to the WEPIC program is unleashing a growing flow of outside grant funds to strengthen and expand the program.

How can we make an overall evaluation of the effects of the program? That should depend on several criteria:

1. the mobilization of large numbers of students and faculty in the program—which has already been achieved—and which continues to grow.
2. the impacts on the community. Some of these such as improvements in health, nutrition, the reduction of violence, and increases in employment are being measured but more time must elapse before trends can be shown.
3. the impact of changes within the schools upon the dedication of pupils to improving their own education will need to be assessed and measured in the future.

For the university, the program has stimulated interdisciplinary research and teaching. Among professors and students, it has improved the relations among white and black students and professors.

The program has not focused exclusively upon the problems of black young men. Through WEPIC, both sexes are involved, but it may help black young women to see their young men increasingly involved in constructive activities. If the program helps black men to find jobs in health-related fields, that will be an enormous advantage to them.

The program suggests a new role for the federal government in dealing with the problems of the inner cities. Secretary of Housing and Urban

Development, Henry G. Cisneros, has strongly endorsed the Penn approach to urban development. If that department survives in the future, it may yet find a noncontroversial role for supporting urban development through the universities and schools.

The University of Pennsylvania program demonstrates the feasibility of building a widespread yet concentrated program of applied research that is also designed to yield basic research results and also advances in social theories. The program is already yielding research advances in the measurement of health and nutrition status of low-income African American children. It is laying the baseline for future measurements of changes in mortality and morbidity in this population.

In social theory, the program extends John Dewey's conception of creating community schools that would reform education by deemphasizing rote learning and involving pupils in tasks that have meaning to them and also contribute to community resources. He saw this as a way to build a participative democratic society.

The school he created was a private school, administered by the Department of Education of the University of Chicago. Whatever its merits, the Laboratory School had little impact on public school education in Chicago or elsewhere.

The Penn program links the university with the public schools of Philadelphia. Furthermore, the program is not limited to one school. It is using the Turner Middle School not only as its area of heaviest concentration but as a pilot model for the extension of the program to other schools in Philadelphia. And this spreading reform movement has stimulated adoption or adaptation of that program to other university-community schools linkages elsewhere.

The program has become so appealing as to attract increasing numbers of Penn students and professors. Anthropology students and professors have been involved from the early stages. Frank Furstenberg, a leading professor of sociology, began in 1995 to orient his teaching and research along the lines of participatory action research (PAR), within the WEPIC program. He now sees the future of sociology building on PAR in the framework of collaboration between community schools and universities.

Penn has supplied the model for building democratic participation in our communities. As other universities adopt or adapt the Penn model, that democratic rebuilding process will advance our knowledge of the dynamic possibilities of our society—and will demonstrate the contributions of the behavioral sciences.

———————————◦•◦———————————

Let us see if we can apply what we are learning from my fieldwork to problem areas I have not studied but only followed from the accounts of others. My focus is upon ways in which the various parties can find to work together on solving one of society's major problems: environmental protection.

In preserving the environment, the government plays a necessary role, yet that role often involves regulations that restrict the freedom of individuals, small businesses to do as they wish with their properties. How can that problem be resolved? There are increasing public pressures on government to carry out cost- benefit analyses before imposing new restrictions. The problem with that approach is that the costs are those levied on individual or corporate property holders whereas the benefits are assumed to be shared by the whole society.

Can federal and state governments collaborate with local governments in resolving local issues? That would involve government offering financial inducements to stimulate local environmental protection efforts. Let us see how this is being done in the following cases.

Edward Cohen-Rosenthal, Director of Cornell University's Work and Environment Initiative, has organized an environmental and community development program in an industrial/residential district along the Baltimore waterfront. They have completed a baseline study of the requirements and facilities for recycling and other means of pollution control. With widespread participation in discussions with representatives of business firms and with residential groups the program has developed plans for protecting the environment while securing greater employment opportunity for higher wage jobs for African-American residents in the new enterprises spurred by dealing with the environmental problems. This program is supported in part by a federal grant designed to support local people in their environmental efforts.

In efforts to control floods on the Mississippi River, the Army Corps of Engineers and state governments have been expending enormous sums to build levees. If these structures protect people and properties where they are built, they nevertheless accelerate the flow of flood waters downstream, just transferring greater problems to downstream areas.

As W. K. Stevens reported (*The New York Times*, August 8, 1995), the Clean Water Act requires developers to create an acre or more of wetlands for each acre they drain. Research along the watershed indicates that new methods of wetland development could drastically reduce floods.

As the government offers financial inducements to encourage the development of new and improved wetlands, private developers are organizing new firms to accelerate this development. In this way, the need to build and restore levees and dikes that are overwhelmed in great floods may one day be sharply reduced or eliminated—thus benefiting citizens, local and state governments, and the federal government.

An unusual cooperative program has linked together the federal, state, and New York City governments with farmers whose lands are located along the newly completed Pepacton reservoir. The water supply for the City is drawn from upstate reservoirs like this one (*The New York Times*, August 13, 1995).

There had been a long-standing adversarial relationship between the farmers and New York City. Farmers believed that the city had violated its promises to farmers for their losses in the development of these reservoirs.

Now the federal government was about to impose new restrictions on the use of agricultural land, to protect the ecology. These regulations could have required farmers to keep their cattle off large areas along those waterways. The set-asides could have been so drastic as to force many farmers out of business.

The governments and the farmers have now found a way out of this impasse.

Forged from the grass roots, the $35.2 million program is one of the nation's first field test of the theory that local, flexible efforts to cut pollution can be more effective than top-down, by-the-book regulation. It is also being held out by Federal agricultural officials as a national model for urban- rural cooperation.

For farmers, the incentive is an average of $75,000 per farm for improvements that cut pollution and, in most cases, improve production, like cement liners that keep the manure in barnyards and grassy buffers that absorb nutrients from animal waste. As Thomas Hutson, a farmer from the...watershed, put it, "We've made some changes that are not only an improvement environmentally, but hopefully will help my bottom line."

With this program, Federal EPA officials decided that it would not be necessary to enforce the order requiring the city to build a $6 billion filtration system. State officials from both the Cuomo and Pataki administrations played key roles, along with Mayor Giuliani of the City. The Water Resources Institute at Cornell University has been involved throughout, monitoring the improvement in water quality.

This has been a prime example of the combination of joint-pay off relations and multi-objective planning. The local farmers and the government of New York City have all benefited. Federal EPA officials have benefited in observing their new policies paying off. And all the parties have been gaining through this learning experience, in ways that could be transferred to other problems.

I am not suggesting that every problem of environmental regulation can be resolved through finding cooperative solutions, but I am suggesting a different way of looking at these problems. Before engaging in political struggles, the parties should look first to see whether a cooperative approach is worth trying.

These days political debates are carried on as if there were only two forces in play: business and government. We need to recognize that there are a number of forces involved that are neither government agencies nor businesses. They go under the name of Non-Governmental Organizations (NGOs) and encompass a wide variety of organizations, including universities, private charity and community development organizations, citizen organizations to protect the environment, or other social and economic causes.

We have already seen some of the roles the universities can play in the Penn WEPIC program and in our discussion of the Baltimore harbor environmental and economic development program under the direction of Edward Cohen-Rosenthal of Cornell University. He is a member of the staff of Programs for Employment and Workplace Systems (PEWS) in the extension division of the School of Industrial and Labor Relations.

Many of these NGOs have arisen from citizen initiative to bring people together to promote a common cause.

We observed a case of this nature in Guatemala, as we were studying the Instituto de Ciencia y Tecnologia Agricolas (ICTA). In one area, the ICTA people found that small farmers had been involved with a project organized by World Neighbors (an NGO based in Oklahoma). Two members of World Neighbors had been studying the agriculture in this village and had been teaching villagers modern methods of contour plowing and mulching and raising crops that enriched the soil. By the time we arrived at this village, World Neighbors had left, but two young villagers trained by them had taken over the commitment to work with village farmers and carry out experiments on their fields. ICTA people were so impressed with their performance that they put them on the ICTA payroll to collaborate with ICTA technicians in managing agronomic trials throughout the community. The indigenous leaders were able to manage 60 agronomic trials a year compared to 25 carried out by the technicians.

This proved to be a very efficient arrangement. The farmer leaders accomplished more trials than the technicians at a much lower salary cost. ICTA did not have to pay the salaries of technically trained people and reward them with hardship pay for working far away from any major city—the village leaders were working where they wanted to live. By 1979 the paraprofessionals were working with several other villages and with two large farm cooperatives. They were also stimulating exchanges of information and ideas among farmers in these various villages.

As I learned later from an NGO publication of the Inter-American Foundation (*Grassroots Development, 19*(1) 1995), paraprofessional farmers, stimulated by World Neighbors, are now spreading the message of local democratic development of people and resources, in collaboration with professionals in agriculture and the behavioral sciences, throughout large areas of Mexico and Honduras.

This linking of grassroots activity with governmental programs shows the possibility of greatly increasing the effectiveness of those programs. What farmers learn from other farmers helps further to accelerate local economic development.

In working with private business, NGOs are showing some promise in resolving environmental protection problems. For example, the Environmental Defense Fund got together with the McDonald Company leaders to devise ways of reducing the mountains of trash produced by the firm's 9,000 U.S. restaurants. The fast food giant has reduced its solid waste output by 7,500 tons of packaging annually over 3 years (*Grass Roots Development, 19*(2), 1995).

A community development NGO, Bronx 2000, has developed an ingenious program in the South Bronx area of New York City, led by

David M. Muchnik through his Big City Forest Company (Andrew C. Revkin in *The New York Times*, March 5, 1997). This business operation turns wood pallets used in shipping large products into New York into new products, producing new jobs.

Big City Forest pays 75¢ for each pallet dropped at the doors of its factory, whereas companies have been paying fees up to $5 from carting companies to take the pallets away.

> Enjoying a rare luxury in the business world, it [Big City Forest] thus gets money not only from its products, but also from the companies supplying its raw material.
>
> By transforming lowly pallets into valuable products in a single operation, Big City Forest is also creating dozens of new jobs...giving previously unemployed people a marketable skill.

Large pallet recycling plants around the country turn the pallets into chips. In that form, the wood is worth about $30 a ton. As flooring, its value rises to $1,200 a ton, and as furniture, the wood in the pallets is worth about $6,000 a ton, according to a Big City environment specialist.

The least valuable woods are used for new pallets. The scraps left are burned in the factory furnace to heat the buildings. The more valuable wood is used for the manufacture of flooring and furniture. The company trains its workforce of about 24 people and expects to triple that number within 3 years.

Mr. Muchnik is hoping to franchise this operation into many cities. On the benefits to the total society, he estimates that nearly half of the wood cut down from hardwood trees in the country could be saved, if similar operations were created throughout the country.

Big City Forest has created an extraordinary joint-payoff situation for companies, cities, and the nation.

This involvement of NGOs with business has not as yet been as extensive and effective as it has been with government, but the principles involved should be equally effective in both areas. The NGO enters the scene to provide information and put pressure on those in power. Then the NGO seeks to establish a collaborative relationship through offering assistance in solving problems affecting business, citizens, and their government.

As *The New York Times* (May 27, p. 10) reported, the Environmental Protection Agency (EPA) is now negotiating new environmental plans with major corporations, such as Intel, for example. Management of the corporation agrees to process its waste products to meet a higher standard than official regulations require. If the EPA approves the plan and faithfully carries it out, management is free from the burden of constantly applying for waivers whenever its production processes change. This enables the company to gain major savings in time and money over what it would cost going through the regular regulatory process.

Let me conclude with two problems for which I now have no leads for solutions and which therefore seem to me to require major efforts in applied research, (a) the widening income gap between the top and bottom income earners—since the 1970s the U.S. has become the most *unequal* society among western industrialized nations, and (b) the loss of what economist Robert Putnam calls *social capital*.

The first problem is increasingly recognized; the second problem is only now beginning to get some attention. In recent years, parents are spending less time with their children or are with them simply watching television rather than engaging in joint activities. With more mothers having to work to keep up family income or because young women now are seeking the same career opportunities as men, mothers necessarily spend less time with their children. When they are at home with their children, they are so exhausted with household chores that they are inclined to use the TV as a convenient babysitter.

In recent years, there has been a decline in membership in all sorts of voluntary activities, from Parent Teachers Associations (PTAs) to service clubs and to labor unions. It is striking to note that, although more people than ever are bowling, there has been a sharp decline in participation in bowling leagues.

This apparent loss in social capital may have far-reaching effects from the local community to the national scene. Are people losing the capacity to get together to seek joint solutions to their problems and instead blaming each other for their problems? If that indeed is the trend, can anything be done to reverse it?

Perhaps the revitalization of labor unions now being attempted by a new reform leadership holds promise. We see unions now investing more time and money in training organizers and also devoting more attention to studying current and recent efforts to determine better what works and what does not work.

———————————————•◦•———————————————

In concluding these reflections on a vision for sociology and society, let me propose a somewhat different approach to a diagnosis of our problems and a potential line of solutions.

Way back in the 1920s, sociologist William F. Ogburn presented the cultural lag hypothesis: the idea that technological changes were occurring faster than cultural changes. He assumed that this disequilibrium was creating social, economic, and cultural problems.

If that was the underlying problem in the 1920s, it must be much more acute in the 1990s when the pace of technological changes has become far faster than in the early years of this century. But that diagnosis is of no use to us unless it leads to some avenues of solution. Let me propose my line of approach.

Humans are not only creative in technological ways; they also are *social inventors*. We need now to find ways to accelerate the rate of social inventions and their diffusion and concentration on certain key social and economic problems.

To illustrate, let us focus on the environment, since that brings together many interrelated problems. The Republicans, who captured control of the House of Representatives in 1994, assumed they had a mandate to curb the regulatory power of the EPA. As the political debates wore on and reached into the Senate, it became evident that there was widespread support for the environmental controls of the EPA, and the political result was a stalemate. Nevertheless, EPA officials themselves were looking for better ways to protect the environment rather than regulation by the federal government. Government policies now shifted more toward providing incentives than toward enforcing penalties. This shift opened the way to new local level initiatives.

The Baltimore harbor project illustrates some of the possibilities of this new approach. The Cornell Environmental Initiative began by getting representatives of all the stake holders in the local area for discussions on the needs and objectives to be met and served in the area. The first step was to hold a search conference among representatives of the local citizens, the business management interests, the interests of the labor unions, and the local governments of Baltimore and the county. The search conference is a social invention developed by Australian behavioral scientists Merrelyn and Fred Emery (1993). It is an ideal methodology for getting a variety of diverse people together to consider their needs and interests.

The local residents, predominantly poor black people, were particularly interested in new and better employment possibilities. Labor union officials shared these interests and wanted to push for the development of jobs well above the federal minimum wage. The management people were particularly concerned with finding better ways of disposing of their waste projects and were prepared to support a feasibility study of establishing a new firm in the area to gather all the waste generated and, so far as possible, transform it into marketable products, as well as eliminating much of their waste disposal expense. City and county officials were interested in the reduction of environmental pollution and the creation of new jobs and enterprises and new local revenues. EPA officials looked upon this as an important test case for their new incentive approach and were prepared to support it.

Moving ahead with such a broad ranging project is still an unfinished story at this writing, but the outlines of the project are now clear. This is an attempt to create a new social invention, a project bringing together all the stake holders in an urban area under the umbrella of protection and improvement of the environment. It involves development of new social processes of community economic and social development.

If this project succeeds, its lessons can be transferred to many industrial areas around the country. As efforts are made to pursue this line of social research and planning, this presents a vital new area for the focus of applied social research. The Big City Forest Company might well serve as the center piece to such new models.

Note that this proposed line of research builds on some of my theoretical ideas: the centrality of social inventions, the development of joint-payoffs, and multi-objective planning. For environmental studies and also for efforts in other fields, human beings are constantly devising new and promising social inventions. As with technological inventions, some of these will not be utilized. The task of research will be to track these new initiatives, to discover what works and what does not, and to further develop theories and practices of community organizing.

This strategy also demands a focus on participatory action research so that people who are confronting problems at work and at home have the essential opportunities to participate in applied research that promises to improve their social and economic situation.

Such a strategy not only holds promise of yielding important new knowledge. It also holds promise of providing a firmer financial base for social and economic research in the future.

Note that this strategy does not fit into any of the conventional ideologies. It can be embraced by those who call themselves conservatives or liberals. It can be supported by industrial management and organized labor. It can build a new sense of community as people from different backgrounds and different needs and interests learn to enjoy working together for common goals.

REFERENCES

Anderson, Elijah
    1978 A Place on the Corner. Chicago: University of Chicago Press.
Barnard, Chester
    1957 Quoted in Scientific American (November)
Blau, Peter
    1955 The Dynamics of Bureaucracy. Chicago: University of
        Chicago Press.
Blumer, Herbert
    1969 Symbolic Interactionism: Perspective and Method. Englewood
        Cliffs, NJ: Prentice–Hall.
Bridgman, P.W.
    1927 The Logic of Modern Physics. New York: Macmillan.
Dalton, Melville
    1959 Men Who Manage. New York: John Wiley.
Denzin, Norman K.
    1992 Whose Cornerville is it Anyway? Journal of Contemporary
        Ethnography 21(1):120-132.
    1994 The Art and Politics of Interpretation. *In* Handbook of
        Qualitative Research. Norman K. Denzin and Yvonna S.
        Lincoln, eds. Pp. 500–515. Newbury Park, CA: Sage
        Publications.
    1996 The Facts and Fictions of Qualitative Inquiry. Qualitative
        Inquiry 2(2):230.
Emery, Merrelyn
    1996 The Search Conference: A Powerful Method for
        Organizational Change and Community Action. San Francisco:
        Jossey-Bass.

Espinosa, Waldemar
    1973 Las Huancas, Aliados de la Conquista. Lima: Casa de la
    Cultura.
Etzioni, Amitai
    1988 The Moral Dimension. New York: The Free Press.
Gouldner, Alvin
    1960 The Norm of Reciprocity. American Sociological Review
    25(2):161-178.
Greenwood, D. G., and José Luis Gonzalez
    1989 Culturas de Fagor: Estudio Antropologico de las Cooperativas
    de Mondragón. San Sebastian, Spain.
Greenwood, D., W. F. Whyte, and Ira Harkavy
    1993 Participatory Action Research as a Process and as a Goal.
    Human Relations 46(2).
Hall, Richard
    1991 Organizational Behavior. 5th ed. Englewood Cliffs, NJ:
    Prentice-Hall.
Hayes, R. H., S. C. Wheelwright, and K. B. Clark
    1988 Dynamic Manufacturing: Creating the Learning
    Organization. New York: The Free Press.
Homans, George C.
    1950 The Human Group. New York: Harcourt Brace Jovanovich.
    1961 Social Behavior: Its Elementary Forms. New York: Harcourt
    Brace Jovanovich.
Horowitz, Ruth
    1983 Honor and the American Dream. New Brunswick, NJ:
    Rutgers University Press.
Kayser, Thomas J.
    1990 Mining Group Gold: How to Cash in on the Brain Power of a
    Group. El Segundo, CA: Serif Publishing.
Kennedy, Timothy
    1969 The Sky River Project. Unpublished Cornell University
    doctoral dissertation.
Klingel, Sally, and Ann Martin
    1989 A Fighting Chance. Ithaca, NY: ILR Press.

Lawrence, Paul, and Jay Lorsch
    1967 Organization and Environment: Managing Differentiation
        and Integration. Boston: Harvard Graduate School of Business.
Liebow, Eliot
    1967 Tally's Corner. Boston: Little Brown.
Martinez, A.
    1991 El Grup Cooperatiu de Valencia. Editorial de Valencia.
Mauss, Marcel
    1954 The Gift. Glencoe, IL: The Free Press.
Mayr, E.
    1983 The Growth of Biological Thought. Cambridge, MA:
        Harvard University Press.
Merton, Robert K.
    1936 The Unanticipated Consequences of Purposive Action.
        American Sociological Review 1(1):894-904.
Morgan, David, and Liz Stanley, eds.
    1993 Debates in Sociology. Manchester University Press (U.S.
        distributor: New York: St. Martin's Press.)
Richardson, Laurel
    1992 Trash on the Corner: Ethics and Ethnography. Journal of
        Contemporary Ethnography 21(1):103-119.
Roy, Donald
    1959 Banana Time. Human Organization 18(4).
Samuelson, Paul
    1967 Foundations of Economic Analysis. New York: Atheneum.
Schon, Donald
    1983 The Reflective Practitioner. New York: Basic Books.
Skinner, B. F.
    1971 Beyond Freedom and Dignity. New York: Knopf.
Thorsrud, Einar
    1977 Democracy at Work: Norwegian Experience with
        Non-Bureaucratic Forms of Organization. Journal of Applied
        Behavioral Science 13(3):410-421.
Tichy, Neil
    1983 Managing Technique, Politics and Cultural Dynamics. New
        York: John Wiley.

Trist, Eric, and K. W. Bamforth
  1951 Some Social and Psychological Consequences of the Longwall Method of Coal Getting. Human Relations 4:3-38.
Vidich, Arthur
  1992 Boston's North End: An American Epic. Journal of Contemporary Ethnography 21(1):80-102.
Westbrook, Robert B.
  1991 John Dewey and American Democracy. Ithaca, NY: Cornell University Press.
Whyte, William F.
  1943 Street Corner Society. Chicago: University of Chicago Press.
  1949 The Social Structure of the Restaurant. American Journal of Sociology 54(1).
  1951 Pattern for Industrial Peace. New York: Harpers and Brothers.
  1953 Leadership and Group Participation. Bulletin 21: New York State School of Industrial and Labor Relations.
  1955a Money and Motivation. New York: Harpers and Brothers.
  1955b Street Corner Society. 2nd ed. Chicago: University of Chicago Press.
  1963 Culture, Industrial Relations and Economic Development: The Case of Peru. Industrial and Labor Relations Review.
  1969 Organizational Behavior: Theory and Application. Homewood, IL: Richard D. Irwin & Dorsey Press.
  1972 Pigeons, Persons and Piece Rates. Psychology Today (April).
  1981 Street Corner Society. 3rd ed. Chicago: University of Chicago Press.
  1989 Advancing Scientific Knowledge Through Participatory Action Research. Sociological Forum 4(3):367-385.
  1990 The New Manufacturing Organization: Problems and Opportunities for Employee Involvement and Collective Bargaining. National Productivity Review 9(3).
  1991 Social Theory for Action: How Individuals and Organizations Learn to Change. Newbury Park, CA: Sage Publications.
  1993 Street Corner Society. 4th ed. Chicago: University of Chicago Press.
  1994 Participant Observer. Ithaca, NY: ILR Press.

1996 Facts, Interpretations, and Ethics in Qualitative Inquiry. Qualitative Inquiry 2(2):242.
1996 Qualitative Sociology and Deconstructionism. Qualitative Inquiry 2(2):220.

Whyte, W. F., ed.
1990 Participatory Action Research. Beverly Hills, CA: Sage Publications.

Whyte, W. F., and Giorgio Alberti
1976 Power, Politics, and Progress: Social Change in Rural Peru. New York: Elsevier.

Whyte, W. F., and R. R. Braun
1968 On Language and Culture. *In* Institutions and The Person. H. S. Becker, ed. Chicago: Aldine.

Whyte, W. F., B. B. Gardner, and A. H. Whiteford
1946 From Conflict to Cooperation. Applied Anthropology 5(4).

Whyte, W. F., Davydd Greenwood, and Peter Lazes
1989 Participatory Action Research: Through Practice to Science in Social Research. American Behavioral Scientist 32(5):513-551.

Whyte, W. F., and Kathleen K. Whyte
1989 Making Mondragón: the Growth and Dynamics of the Worker Cooperative Complex. Ithaca, NY: ILR Press.
1991 Making Mondragón: the Growth and Dynamics of the Worker Cooperative Complex. 2nd ed. Ithaca, NY: ILR Press.

Whyte, W. F., and Lawrence K. Williams
1963 Supervisory Leadership: An International Comparison. Symposium 33, 1-8 C.I.O.S. International Management Congress XIII.
1968 Toward an Integrated Theory of Development: Economic and Non-Economic Variables in Rural Development. Ithaca, NY: New York State School of Industrial and Labor Relations.

Woodward, J.
1965 Industrial Organization: Theory and Practice. London: Oxford University Press.

INDEX